CREATIVE TEACHING:
MATHEMATICS IN THE
EARLY YEARS AND
PRIMARY CLASSROOM

Related titles:

Creative Teaching: English in the Early Years and Primary Classroom
Chris Horner and Vicki Ryf
978-1-84312-260-9

Creative Teaching: Science in the Early Years and Primary Classroom
Ann Oliver
978-1-84312-259-6

Creative Teaching: History in the Primary Classroom
Rosie Turner-Bisset
978-1-84312-115-8

CREATIVE TEACHING: MATHEMATICS IN THE EARLY YEARS AND PRIMARY CLASSROOM

Mary Briggs with Sue Davis

Routledge
Taylor & Francis Group

LONDON AND NEW YORK

First published 2008 by Routledge
2 Park Square, Milton Park, Abingdon, Oxon, OX14 4RN

Simultaneously published in the USA and Canada
by Routledge
270 Madison Ave, New York, NY 10016

Reprinted 2008

Routledge is an imprint of the Taylor & Francis Group, an informa business

Typeset in Celeste by RefineCatch Limited, Bungay, Suffolk
Printed and bound in Great Britain by TJ International, Padstow, Cornwall

British Library Cataloguing in Publication Data
A catalogue record for this book is available from the British Library

Library of Congress Cataloging in Publication Data
Briggs, Mary (Mary J.)
    Creative teaching : mathematics in the early years and primary classroom / Mary Briggs with Sue Davis.
        p. cm.
    Includes index.
    1. Mathematics–Study and teaching (Elementary)–Great Britain.   I. Davis, Sue.   II. Title.
    QA135.6.B738 2008
    372.7–dc22
                                                                                        2007023595

ISBN 10: 1-84312-462-9
ISBN 13: 978-1-84312-462-7

Contents

Introduction 1

1 Not just a tick or a cross 13

2 Curriculum constraints and possibilities 25

3 Starting points for creative teaching 36

4 The end of death by worksheet: being creative rather than
using worksheets 46

5 Role-play 56

6 Stories and other literature sources 68

7 Writing about mathematics 82

8 Games and other similar activities 99

9 Display and the classroom environment 111

10 Field trips for mathematics 125

11 The sky's the limit 137

References 147

Index 151

Introduction

What do you associate with creativity? How might you describe creativity? What behaviours would you associate with being a creative person?

Task

Before you read any further jot down some initial responses to these initial questions.

We asked two different groups of people. The first were a group of undergraduate students. Here are a few of their answers (Figure 0.1).

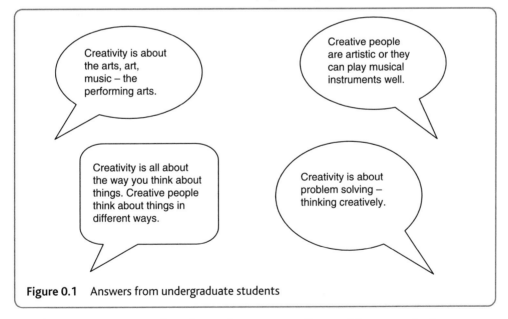

Creativity is about the arts, art, music – the performing arts.

Creative people are artistic or they can play musical instruments well.

Creativity is all about the way you think about things. Creative people think about things in different ways.

Creativity is about problem solving – thinking creatively.

Figure 0.1   Answers from undergraduate students

What is interesting is that the performing arts featured in every single response from the adults here. Most focused on art, music, dance and drama. A few of the responses mentioned thinking skills and the ability to think differently about ideas or events. These were after the initial responses focusing on the performing arts.

The children who were asked about creativity also focused on children being good at art, music or other performing arts (Figure 0.2).

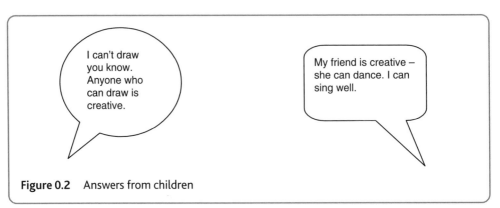

Figure 0.2 Answers from children

The responses from the children and students above indicate that there are some very specific views of creativity and they link to the myths outlined by the Scottish Executive in their work encouraging creativity in Scottish Education.

Myth 1: Creativity is only important in some areas of human activity.

Myth 2: The creative process just happens it is always inspirational effortless and comes like a bolt out of the blue.

Myth 3: Creative people are somehow special, different from the rest of us and actually a bit strange in someway.

(Scottish Executive 2000)

Other research studies focusing on creativity have concentrated on a variety of different foci as can be seen in the following examples:

- creative people, their qualities and traits as being creative (Stein 1984, Cropley 2001)
- the creativity of how people interact with the environment (Meyer 1999)
- exploring the detail of the creative work undertaken (Policastro and Gardner 1999)
- exploring how society impacts upon creativity.

(Gardner 1993)

For the most part these studies also focus on the original and unique creative people and the outcomes. For people like Einstein, who Gardner (1993) writes about, indicate that the evidence of their creative thinking came outside the formal education system. Einstein was not recognised as even good at mathematics whilst at school which, for teachers, is an interesting fact to consider about the identification of creativity within the individual.

However, the general view of creativity is that it is important in the arts areas and few people mention the creative process in relation to mathematics and science subjects. Problem solving is sometimes linked to creativity and yet this is a separate area of exploration. A learner can be creative in relation to problem solving but this is not to be viewed as the same as creative mathematics. We will explore this aspect in each of the chapters to indicate the differences between problem solving and mathematics.

A more helpful categorisation of the different aspects of creativity comes from Tina Bruce in her description of layers of creativity.

First – Original and world-shaking creativity

Second – Recreating an idea in a different time and place

Third – Specialists who create ideas which are important in their field, who may not be famous, but who contribute in important ways

Fourth – Everyday creativity that makes life worth living

(Bruce 2004)

Task

Think about these different layers of creativity. What would you give as examples for each layer in relation to education? In relation to mathematics?

Bruce's first layer of creativity is clearly not the focus of this book. In relation to mathematics the activities in this realm are the proving of Fermat's last theorem by Andrew Wiles (Singh 1997) for example. These are rare events in mathematics and have effects on the whole world of mathematics. We may find that as a teacher we are teaching a child who goes on to become the next Andrew Wiles and proves another new theorem in mathematics. The second layer of creativity relates to the rediscovery of ideas like helicopters which Leonardo originally designed in the fifteenth century and was developed in the twentieth century. Again this is not the main focus of this book. The third and fourth layers of creativity are definitely the focus of this book. The specialists here are both the teachers and children teaching and learning mathematics. Although you may not consider either of these two groups as specialists we would argue that, as learning is an important process for life, children learning mathematics gives them ideas about their world and they therefore contribute to society in important ways. The teachers are either specialists in teaching a specific age group or in the subject of mathematics and are therefore contributing to others' (the children's) understanding of that subject and that is equally important. The fourth layer of creativity is the focus of creativity in classrooms and early years settings on an everyday basis and may be seen in relation to the preparation for teaching, the actual teaching, the learning and/or the responses of the children.

Before we explore each of these in detail throughout this book it is important to say that we are exploring teaching creativity. We would agree with the Scottish Executive approach that:

> Creativity is nurtured, not taught. One of the ambitions of this cultural strategy is to develop the conditions in which creativity and innovation can flourish in all sectors of Scottish life . . . equip pupils with the foundation skills, attitudes and expectations necessary to prosper in a changing society and . . . encourage creativity & ambition.
>
> (Scottish Executive 2000)

These are key aspects of the approach the whole of this book takes, exploring the possibilities within mathematics teaching and learning without prescribing a specific way to do things. We hope that this book will make the reader rethink the teaching and learning of mathematics and see the potential creativity within the subject.

> **Task**
>
> Before we move on, take a few minutes to consider what you think it means to be creative in mathematics? Is it possible to be creative in mathematics? Do you see yourself as mathematically creative?

Now let's look at the development of creativity in relation to mathematics, starting with very young children.

Young children's creativity outside the arts

Creativity in mathematics starts even before children arrive in a learning environment with others but starts as they explore the world around them. The following is a small example in relation to the development of language in pre-school children.

If you listen to children playing they will invent words for quantities as part of playing with language; language for specific purpose. Mathematics can be seen as language that we learn how to speak. We also learn that precise language can be used to describe situations, events or classify. Two-year-old Alex was overheard trying some of these things out as he was talking to his toys. 'Tigger has a tail . . . Alex has no tail.' This small boy was playing with his classification of objects including self, all part of beginning to think mathematically (Briggs 2005).

Many of the ideas and skills young children learn in play can be early signs of the links between mathematics and creativity. The links may not always appear immediately obvious.

> **Task**
>
> Read the lists of activities below that babies and young children engage in and think about how you see the links with mathematics. You may need to think beyond the activity itself and consider where this leads in relation to children's learning.

Creativity, play and mathematics

Play is a creative activity for children that allows them to explore their environment and make sense of the world around them. They experiment as the following brief outline of activities linking to early mathematics skills and knowledge at different ages illustrates:

Babies

- actions like banging objects on surfaces
- playing common games like 'round and round the garden' – anticipation, prediction
- joy in responding to interactions
- movement patterns (schemas) – experimenting and receiving feedback
- cause and effect – I did that!

Toddlers and young children

- making mental images
- imitation
- developing personal symbols – making one thing to stand for another, whether it is present or not
- pretending.

The babies banging objects on surfaces enables them to begin to classify which surfaces they can hit to make noises and which won't make any noise. This continues to develop into classifying the kind of noises the surfaces make in comparison with each other. Classifying is a mathematical skill they will use with shapes and measures for example later on. Playing games and the ability to predict along with movement patterns will support their geometric skills, and prediction and cause and effect will support algebra and problem solving. The symbolic representation that young children use in their play is a prerequisite for understanding algebraic substitution. Through this we can see that they already have a creative approach to aspects of mathematics without any tuition. Many toys will also allow children to begin to develop through mathematical thinking at this age in creative ways. We might think first of toys like those where the child must fit a shape into a set hole and only the right shapes fit into correct holes. This, however, is quite prescriptive and does not allow for any creativity on the part of the child. The child can achieve the right solution through trial and error and a little patience. It is the toys which allow for a variety of combinations and solutions, like duplo or simple building blocks, which allow more open-ended play activities and therefore also allow for children to develop their creativity in relation to shapes, position and orientation. The shop or similar role play environment allows children to explore their thinking in relation to quantity and money.

You may have overheard children in the shop where a loaf of bread costs a million pounds and you still get change. These children are exploring their own worlds and the mathematics within them.

> **Task**
>
> Now you have seen how we are making the link for the activities that babies engage with, can you see the potential links with those listed for the toddlers and young children?

We must be careful, however, that children do not develop misconceptions as part of their creative exploration of their mathematical world that will create barriers to learning mathematics later in life. Many things which children explore in early life are developed as their experience grows and as they move into a bigger world further from the starting point which is them. An example of this is a counting task by a three-year-old asked if there were enough drinks for her mum, brother and herself. She counted one, two, me, making the whole exercise personal.

Older children and mathematics

As older children learn about mathematics there is a move away from practical starting points for investigating aspects of the subject and a push towards recording. Although the National Numeracy Strategy emphasises oral/mental methods for calculations there is still the pressure for teachers to use other materials such as worksheets. This aspect of use of materials is explored in more detail in Chapter 4. Unfortunately, as children get older there is an expected formality about their learning including recording their work. Older children can be creative learners of mathematics and can be innovative in their approaches to solving problems.

The last statement raises issues about the language we use to describe creativity and creative activities in particular contexts. Craft (2003) discusses how important this issue is as we slip between the use of terms associated with this area and the effects this can have on the values of practice: 'Valuing creative learning, for example, is distinct from valuing creative teaching.'

> ### Task
> Take a moment to consider the words that you might use in connection with creativity in education. You may have included some of the following words: innovation, flair, originality, unique, experimentation, imagination. Consider how you think these apply to mathematics learning and teaching.

What is important about creative learning and teaching of mathematics is that the intention is not to make children subject specialists.

> Thoughtful people want today's child to be 'more mathematically minded', not a mathematician; 'more musically minded' not a musician; 'more scientifically minded' not a scientist; etc. Thoughtful people have always wanted these aims for elementary education. But this is not the same thing as making the child into a mathematician . . .
> (Glennon 1963)

What is interesting is that despite the age of this quotation it is relevant in the current climate of changes to the curriculum and these are discussed in more detail in Chapter 2. The important issue is what we are trying to do in Early Years and primary education. We are not trying to make mathematicians of young children but we want them to appreciate the breadth of mathematics as a subject area. The other aspect which is a current focus is the connection between topics within mathematics and mathematics with other areas of learning/subjects taught to each age group.

Your current teaching

Mathematics is often a subject that is not a favourite for teachers. This is partly based on their own experiences as a learner of mathematics. It is also a subject where teachers feel they need to know the answers. This is explored in more detail in Chapter 1 with views of mathematics as a subject. There are likely to be areas of learning/subjects that you prefer to teach. This is again partly based on your own experiences and the strengths and successes you have had in teaching.

Task

Take a moment to think about your teaching and where you think your strengths lie. What are the strengths of your teaching, regardless of area of learning/subject taught?

This is an important area as this book is intended to provoke reflection on current practice and to think about trying different approaches to teaching and learning in mathematics. It is essential that this begins with the strengths of current practice which you may not be transferring to mathematics at present. The most interesting example of this was a teacher who had amazing skills in facilitating children discussing issues and books in English; however, when mathematics was to be taught the teaching style changed and she liked the control of using scheme materials and worksheets. Part of the issue explored with her was that she did not feel her subject knowledge was strong in mathematics and therefore wanted to control the situation. In English she felt confident and therefore the style of teaching appeared less structured although the teacher had very clear ideas about the direction of the teaching.

Woods' (1990) work on creative teaching identified four major components of creative teachers practice:

- Innovation – these may be favourite activities that you have designed and/or adapted as part of teaching and not just in mathematics.
- Ownership – this is a difficult area for teachers with the extensive guidance given but is explored in more detail in Chapter 2.
- Control – this could be seen as control of the curriculum but it is also about the control of the direction of the teaching. Although activities may be planned, the outcomes may extend into unplanned and unpredictable areas.
- Relevance – the activities and direction of teaching must be relevant to the area of learning and the specific learning expected.

Your current teaching may show examples of creativity in one or more of these areas. The teacher described earlier had most difficulty with the component of control particularly in relation to mathematics yet she was able to use creative teaching methods to great effect in other subjects. You may have strengths in other areas that could be transferred to mathematical development/mathematics which would assist the development of teaching and learning. Table 0.1 offers some suggestions as a starting point for your thinking.

In order for children to be creative, teachers and other adults working with them need to be creative and this has been found to be a barrier to developing creativity in education. It can feel as though this has to be a huge shift but it isn't

Table 0.1 How your teaching strengths could be transferred to mathematics

Strengths	How it may be used at the moment	How this might transfer to mathematics
Facilitating discussions in CLL/English	Using this currently to get children to present their ideas, emphasising speaking and listening	Using the same skills children can be given the opportunity to discuss mathematics activity and tell adults and the rest of the children what they have been doing and what they have learnt. A teacher with these strengths may find Chapters 5, 6 and 7 a helpful starting point.
Science investigations	Planning and teaching children about science investigations, emphasising asking questions, planning and reviewing	Using the same skills employed for investigations for science can be transferred into problem solving, games and investigations in mathematics. A teacher with these strengths may find Chapters 3 and 8 a helpful starting point.
Art and display	A more creative focus for teaching and therefore mathematics doesn't appear to have links with my strengths	Teachers with strengths in the arts can feel that it is more difficult to transfer skills but their knowledge of art, for example, can be seen as useful in Chapter 10 which includes the use of pictures as a starting point for mathematics. A teacher with these strengths may find Chapters 9 and 10 a helpful starting point.
Physical development/PE	An active approach to learning and teaching	Again, having a more physical approach can be an advantage to children who tend towards kinaesthetic learning. A teacher with these strengths may find Chapters 3, 4, 8 and 10 a helpful starting point.

necessary to start thinking in this way. Halliwell (1993) shows that creative teaching is not about the huge changes but suggests that four qualities are required:

- a clear sense of need
- the ability to read the situation
- the willingness to take risks
- the ability to monitor and evaluate events.

Small steps using the strengths you already have are the best starting point and even Ofsted agrees, as is shown by the following quote:

> . . . this report indicates (that) the creativity observed in children is not associated with a radical new pedagogy – though some teachers feel it might be, if only they can find what it is . . . but a willingness to observe, listen and work closely with children to help them develop their ideas in a purposeful way. While the stimulus and structures which enable creativity to happen differ somewhat from subject to subject, this focused engagement with the individual pupil – even within a group situation – is common to all the creative work which HMI observed, and is of course common to all good teaching.
>
> (Ofsted 2003: para 7)

Why is it important to start with the teaching? Children can be creative and adults don't need to be. Teachers and other adults need to see the potential and to guide and support children's creativity especially in areas like mathematics that is not usually seen as creative. Teachers need to provide the stimulus and the appropriate resources to support creative thinking and perhaps, most of all, be prepared to be creative alongside the children.

> Teaching for creativity involves teaching creatively . . . to put it another way, teachers cannot develop the creative abilities of their pupils if their own creative abilities are suppressed.
>
> (NACCCE 1999: 90)

> *Task*
>
> Before you read on further, jot down any issues you can see with the stance that has been taken here. Look back at your strengths and think about how you could build upon these as you are introduced to the ideas in the rest of this book.

About this book

This book is designed to explore both creative learning and creative teaching of mathematics across the Early Years and Primary age range. The authors hope this book will prompt different ways of thinking about mathematics within your educational context. The timing of this book is important as there is a shift in the apparent constraints of teaching and learning of mathematics with a loosening of the controls from the centre. The focus is now on learning rather than teaching which linked to the personalised learning agenda gives credence to a return to a child-centred approach. Children's interests are again important to motivate and stimulate learning. One approach does not suit all. Teachers are more aware and are taking account of different preferred learning styles. Greater emphasis is given to reducing the barriers to children's learning. The result of all this is that different teaching strategies are required to meet the new agenda. For more mature teachers this could feel as though the clock has turned back to the early years of their teaching. For newer teachers trained on the strategies and the accountability this brought with it to specific teaching methods this could be viewed as a massive change. Some of the newer teachers will see these changes as a new challenge which they are able to embrace and develop whilst others may not feel prepared for this way of working. Planning and teaching with links between subjects is not a straight return to the 'topic approach' but takes the best from that approach and mixes it with the best of the approaches from the strategies. It is not intended that this book will give all the answers but will provide a stimulus for developing your practice; the stimulus for development through potential areas of teachers' strengths and through an engagement with questions such as 'Is mathematics creative?', 'What might be potential starting points for creative mathematics teaching?' and 'How might I move away from using worksheets or similar activities?'

The structure of this book allows the reader to dip in and out of the materials presented here in order to support the developments in learning and teaching. You may also find some familiar activities and/or suggestions in the following chapters that will reassure you that creatively teaching mathematics is possible and not outside your reach.

A brief overview of the contents of each chapter is detailed below.

Chapter 1: Not just a tick or a cross
This chapter explores creativity in mathematics and discusses what makes mathematics special.

Chapter 2: Curriculum constraints and possibilities
This chapter looks at the apparent constraints created by the curriculum documentation and guidance materials across the whole age range including unit plans for the numeracy strategy. It also looks at the possibilities emerging from the Primary National Strategy (PNS) that may allow a more creative approach to mathematics and the links between areas of learning/subjects.

Chapter 3: Starting points for creative teaching
This chapter offers some starting points for thinking about a creative approach to teaching mathematics.

Chapter 4: The end of death by worksheet
This chapter looks at why teachers use worksheets and what might be the alternatives to teach creatively.

Chapter 5: Role-play

Although usually associated with early years teaching and learning, this chapter shows how role-play can provide rich environments for children across the age range.

Chapter 6: Stories and other literature sources

This chapter discusses how stories can provide a stimulus for mathematics teaching and learning. How can appropriate stories be chosen to provide sufficient mathematical activity?

Chapter 7: Writing about mathematics

Mathematics is not usually seen as an area where writing is either necessary or encouraged. This chapter discusses the benefits of offering children opportunities to write about mathematics.

Chapter 8: Games and other similar activities

This chapter continues to offer stimuli for creative approaches to teaching mathematics through the use of games and other activities.

Chapter 9: Display and the classroom environment

This chapter explores ways and reasons for displaying mathematics and how to 'mathematise' the environment for children.

Chapter 10: Field trips for mathematics

It is hard to think about a visit to watch mathematicians at work but there are lots of other opportunities to exploit the mathematics in the environment. This chapter looks at focusing field trips of different types on mathematics and how this can give children opportunities to explore mathematics and connections with other areas of knowledge.

Chapter 11: The sky's the limit

This final chapter focuses on what might be the next steps in relation to the development of creative teaching and learning mathematics and how to continue these developments and the resources that are needed.

The authors of this book hope you will enjoy reading the ideas here and begin to notice the mathematical potential around you and the children with whom you work.

CHAPTER 1

Not just a tick or a cross

This chapter will explore some of the issues about the nature of mathematics and the assumptions that it can lead to in relation to the degree of flexibility and creativity that is possible within the domain of mathematics.

The flexibility and the degree to which subjectivity is applied to the teaching and learning of a subject can determine how much creativity is possible. So for the arts subjects there is plenty of opinion about whether an outcome is good or correct. These areas can be difficult to assess as a consequence but often likes and dislikes are related to tastes and personal preferences. Arts subjects are not within rules; skills and knowledge can be taught and learnt but often the final outcomes from children can vary widely. For mathematics the rules are very clear and taught in terms of procedures and knowledge to commit to memory. Conceptual understanding is still important but this is about the connections between aspects of mathematics and how and why the rules and procedures work. One of the main problems for mathematics is that it is either seen as right or wrong. Answers to arithmetic can't really be partly right. As a consequence, mathematics tends to be seen as black or white, right or wrong and therefore there is no room for creativity within mathematics itself.

'Creativity' has, though, been granted official recognition as one of the overarching aims of the curriculum in English schools so this appears to leave a dichotomy when thinking of mathematics. Children are seen to be creative when they are encouraged to make connections between one area of learning and another and so extend their understanding. Effective teaching and learning of mathematics is about making the connections between the aspects of the subject. However there is no one definition of what 'creativity' is and therefore is can be hard to see how this connects to mathematics. This can be seen from the discussion in the Introduction. Sharp (2004) suggests a list of components that are commonly identified as being part of the creative process, which are contrasted in Table 1.1 with the evidence of these components in mathematical learning.

Table 1.1 Creative components and the links with mathematical learning

Creative component	Evidence of this in mathematical learning
Imagination	Imaginative approach to problem solving, calculation strategies, strategies for recalling facts.
Originality	This is a hard component for mathematics but children can create originality in approaches and strategies and 'real-life problem solving'. There is also the issue that when a child finds an answer to a problem for the first time the originality is for the individual rather than for the whole of society.
Productivity	Productivity in the sense of generating a range of ideas and productivity in relation to finding solutions whether or not they are original.
Problem solving	The use and application of knowledge and skills in a variety of situations includes problem solving. In mathematics, problem solving covers three areas: word problems, problems and situations set in a mathematical context but not real, and real-life problem solving.
Production and outcome of value and worth	If mathematics is seen as an inherent 'truth' then there is value and worth in all its outcomes. The outcomes in mathematics are valued for their accuracy. There is also value and worth when children produce outcomes for themselves, leading to pride and increased self-esteem.

Task

Do you agree with the evidence suggested? Could you add evidence? Consider your own views of mathematics. How do you see mathematics? Is it a formal rule-bound subject or is it a flexible and creative way of thinking? What difference do you think your views of mathematics have on the ways you might teach children or work with them on mathematical activities?

The Robinson Report (NACCCE 1999) argues that, while there are strong links between the expressive arts and creativity, viewing creativity as solely or mainly the province of the arts is unhelpful because it can lead to a denial of creativity in science and mathematics. Some of the other concerns in relation to mathematics can be highlighted through Sharp's (2004) compilation of key issues particularly in relation to creativity and the Early Years.

How the creative issues link to mathematics

Creativity is confined to the arts

This continues to support the view that creativity is only for the arts and therefore mathematics is not a creative subject. This provides a very narrow definition of creativity and denies those who provide elegant proofs in mathematics are not being creative nor are those who develop new algorithms for calculations of trends in economics.

Knowledge transfer across domains is unproblematic

Aspects like problem solving are considered part of being creative and yet the transfer of skills and knowledge learnt in mathematical problem solving is not encouraged nor sometimes even acknowledged. Problem solving tend-to be taught as a separate skill outside the work in science and mathematics.

Creativity equals fun

Mathematics is seen as a 'serious' subject. If creativity is fun then it can't be happening in mathematics as that's not fun – it's hard work. Succeeding is always fun and helps to raise self-esteem and confidence.

Creativity is an elite trait, restricted to a few very talented individuals

If this is so, then in terms of mathematics only a very few will be able to engage in creativity; yet, as can seen from some of the examples in this chapter and in the rest of the book, creativity comes in many different forms. We need to move away from creativity in mathematics being seen as the preserve of the more able and gifted and talented even if mathematics itself is seen as an elite subject.

Education for creativity can be provided through unstructured play and unsupported activity

Creative children need creative teachers and adults to encourage and develop their creativity regardless of the subject focus. For the Early Years this can be through play but play activities can be introduced to older children to allow them to explore mathematical ideas through games, puzzles and problems. Children also need time to explore mathematics without adult intervention which allows time to pose the questions themselves and to 'have a go' at activities without always being told there is a specific way to approach an activity. This was a criticism of the earlier problem solving approaches which taught a specific rubric of how to solve problems. This rubric then became the new problem solving procedure. This kind of approach did not even allow for sometimes initial exploration by the children without intervention.

Creativity does not require a high level of subject knowledge

Again, part of the problem with mathematics is that it can seem like you only get to the 'interesting parts' of the subject after you have completed all the 'dull' stuff. The very creative research mathematicians do require a high level of subject knowledge but solving problems, puzzles and even considering different strategies for calculation does not require high levels of subject knowledge and can be shown by the activities of very young children. Solving 'regular' problems is a creative act even when the solutions are already known. This is a creative activity for the individual. Sometimes knowledge can be a barrier to looking at problems in different or novel ways. A half-remembered solution or approach can be a real block to establishing any effective approach.

Task

Do you remember half-remembering an approach or a specific problem or activity when faced with the same situation later? Try to recall the feelings at the time and what these meant for potentially blocking your work on the activity. How might they be avoided with children?

Mathematics is often used by other subjects to support the truth of experimentation in science, psychology and geography, for example. If ideas can be proved mathematically then they are considered true. The following gives an overview of the different aspects of mathematics.

Mathematics

Knowledge

- number facts
- multiplication tables
- rules
- procedures
- routines
- definitions

Processes

- questioning
- using and applying existing mathematics knowledge in different contexts

Skills

- hypothesising
- reasoning and deducting
- extrapolating
- remembering
- reflecting
- classifying
- comparing
- ordering
- choosing appropriate tools for measuring
- predicting

Attitudes and beliefs

- mathematics is not just a utilitarian subject
- mathematics can be fun
- mathematics can be achievable
- mathematics is both a knowledge-based and an enquiry-based discipline

Whose perspective?

Sometimes it is not the child's perspective on the situation but it can be the adult's interventions that create the difficulties. A scenario in a reception class involved encouraging the children to add quantities together. The whole class was sitting in a circle. Two dice were then thrown and the children asked to add the two lots of dots together. On one occasion the dice were thrown and the faces showed 5 dots and 4 dots. One child quickly said there were 9 altogether. This was apparently without counting all the dots. The pupil was not asked to explain how he had arrived at the answer, but the teacher asked the child to count to make sure. The child then focused on counting all the dots on both dice.

After this incident the teacher explained her reason for asking the child to count the dots as a way of demonstrating to the rest of the class, who wouldn't all necessarily have been able to do this as quickly, and needed to focus on the process of counting. In this example the child was thinking and acting creatively beyond the expectations of the teacher. The class had not been taught to count on and were still at the 'count all' stage with calculating totals of two quantities. The child was not rewarded for his creative approach to the situation but was in fact taken back to a previous strategy used. This is not a criticism of the teacher, who made a pragmatic decision on their actions based upon the needs of the whole class rather than the individual. It is an opportunity to reflect upon an example of what happens in busy classrooms. It is not clear what effect the actions had on the child's perception of his response to the question asked. Taking a child back to use a previous strategy may have had the effect of placing a ceiling on the child's calculating.

> **Task**
>
> Think of a situation where a child's responses have surprised you in mathematics and how you have reacted to this. Did the child demonstrate aspects of creativity beyond the current levels of teaching and/or learning in the class?

Young children and their use of creativity in mathematics

Young children often include humour in their creative approaches to their tasks. One example of this involved a class of children working on riddles and a little girl posed the following riddle: 'What has 25 legs and is stuck in mud?' All those around were completely baffled and tried lots of different guesses. At first they thought the little girl had got the number of legs wrong as this didn't appear to fit any known situation. One of the adults sitting with the children asked another group of children across to listen to the riddle and offer their suggestions. One boy said that he knew immediately what the answer was: 'That's easy – it's a spider with too many legs stuck in the mud because he has no wellies!' The little girl who was obviously on the same wavelength said 'That's right' and started to giggle. Again this situation shows that it can be difficult to find out what children are thinking.

> **Task**
>
> Think about occasions when children use humour as part of their response to activities in mathematics. How could you build upon that within your teaching to support and encourage their mathematical thinking?

The more able and gifted

Mathematical creativity is sometimes seen as only the province of the most able or gifted. This is partly as a result of the view that you need to have a great deal of mathematics subject knowledge to be creative within the subject. This is something only research mathematicians do. Yet already in this chapter there are examples of children's approaches to being creative within mathematics. The ability to think and use strategies flexibly is a key skill to becoming a confident and successful mathematician as the work of Tall *et al.* (2001) shows. Although the more able and gifted are not the only group capable of demonstrating creativity in mathematics it is within this group of children that it may be more immediately evident. This is partly because of the kinds of activities this group of children are given to do. The following extract is from some work looking at the approaches taken by the more able and the gifted children in Y6 (Wilson and Briggs 2002). The problem they were asked to solve was:

a and b are whole numbers. What could they be?

$$a \div b = 4.125$$

Sam and Ben had been identified as gifted by their teacher. They responded strategically to this task identifying 0.125 as one eighth directly:

'You could times that by something. Like 4.125 times by 2. It has to be whole numbers. Times by 8 . . . That's what one eighth is' (Sam, gifted)

'It would probably have to be 8 . . . because $8 \times 1.25 = 10$ . . .' (Ben, gifted)

The insight of these pupils in exploiting connections resulted in elegant and concise solutions. These examples exemplify the observed tendency of the gifted to plan a strategy that results in an efficient and elegant solution.

Task

Look for children exploiting connections and producing the elegant and concise solutions whether that is in practical play activities, mental calculations or written activities.

Problems with creative approaches by children and what they might mean

Creativity in mathematics by children can lead to two distinctly different outcomes if the creativity is not immediately apparent. The following are two scenarios to illustrate this specific issue.

Child A The child has been asked to write the numbers between 4 and 16. Figure 1.1 is the result.

Figure 1.1   Numbers between 4 and 16

What is interesting about this example is that, at first glance, a teacher might say that this child has clear problems with writing numerals and may be dyscalculic or dyslexic. The response from the child is even more surprising. The child said that she was bored with the task and had therefore written the numbers so you could read them in the mirror as it made the task more interesting. The match between the expectations of the teacher setting the task and the child's abilities could be questioned. It also brings into question the learning styles and interest levels within the task. If we were just looking at the outcomes our response to this as a teacher could take us away from the issues underlying the initial response by the child. Here, creativity masked the child's true abilities and without the conversation could have resulted in labelling her as a problem.

> **Task**
>
> Have you encountered what you might have initially seen as an awkward response to a mathematics task? Have you been able to explore the response further with the learner?

Child B This child was asked to calculate 12 + 23 and gave an answer of 8.

> **Task**
>
> Think about your initial response to this answer. What kinds of things do you find you are considering?

Here the child has added all the digits together without taking into account place value. At one level you might look at this and consider this a clear misconception or lack of understanding of rules of arithmetic. Without a discussion with the child it is not possible to interpret exactly what is going on. A teacher may have a number of ideas which may well influence the questioning of this child or subsequent tasks given to discover the true reason for this response.

This brings us back to one of the issues introduced at the beginning of the chapter and that is mathematics being seen as right or wrong. Methods of calculation can be varied but they need to be generalisable and they need to give a correct answer. Children's own methods can be laborious and therefore lack the efficiency that is expected of competent calculators. For teachers and others working with young children the challenge is to give support; a balance between children developing their own methods and ensuring that they can actually work out calculations correctly and therefore positively enhance their self-esteem. Working on own methods and getting calculations incorrect can have a significantly negative effect on self-esteem and relationship with the subject. If there are negative feelings about the subject there will be limited confidence to become creative with the material.

Being a mathematician

Being creative is not about every child becoming a mathematician but it is worth looking at the creativity in their roles in order to understand how mathematics can be seen as creative. Mathematicians develop theorems and they have therefore created something. Although these are abstract they are creations and, as a result, creative.

Creative thinking

Another way to look at the creative process in relation to mathematics is to explore the idea of 'creative thinking'.

Willings (1980) identifies three kinds of 'creative thinking':

- Adaptive thinking – the ability to relate what is observed to something to which it is not obviously relatable (making links between apparently unconnected areas)
- Elaborative thinking – researching, refining and often beautifying the ideas of some other thinker
- Developmental thinking – enables the individual to enlarge his (sic) concept of himself and the world around him.

How well do you think this offers an explanation for the creativity possible in mathematics since mathematics is about thinking and making connections between aspects of the subject and the real world? It is also being able to move from the concrete and real to the abstract where working with symbols alone is expected. This shift from concrete to abstract thinking and understanding may also allow greater creativity as . . . 'When thinking is based on simple concrete information, creativity is limited to simple departures from the usual. Thinking based on abstract complex properties, on the other hand, allows higher levels of generalization and abstraction . . .' (Cropley 2001). This implies that mathematics is indeed a creative subject which emphasises generality and abstraction.

The QCA materials *Creativity: find it, promote it* explores some general areas that they consider helpful in promoting creativity. The skills they see as important are:

- questioning and challenging
- making connections and seeing relationships
- envisaging what might be
- exploring ideas, keeping options open
- reflecting critically on ideas, actions and outcomes.

(QCA 2004)

Within mathematics it is possible to question and challenge; why does this procedure work? Challenge can be created for children to apply the knowledge and skills learnt in mathematics sessions and lessons either to other situations in mathematics or across the curriculum. Making connections is a really important part of success with mathematics so that knowledge and skills can be flexibly applied. Seeing relationships is an important part of early algebraic skills. In problem solving and investigations, envisaging is an important skill to develop. Spatial awareness can be enhanced through developing visualisation and specifically being able to visualise shape and space relationships. Visualisation is described as 'the ability to represent, transform, generate, communicate, document, and reflect on visual information' (Hershkowitz 1989). Exploring the generation, transformation and communication of ideas should be part of the process of teaching and learning mathematics. Reflecting critically on ideas, actions and outcomes can be part of any mathematical activity. Why does it perhaps still not feel that mathematics is a subject area that allows creativity from the learners' perspective?

Task

Consider the creative thinking described above. How does this fit with your conceptions of mathematics learning and teaching? What if any are the issues for you?

Mathematics problem

The reason for this difficulty is a result of how mathematics is viewed both in our society and within education. Mathematics as a subject has an image problem. It is seen as bound by rules and procedures yet the guidance teachers and other adults are given about mathematics does include:

> Mathematics is a creative discipline. It can stimulate moments of pleasure and wonder when a pupil solves a problem for the first time, discovers a more elegant solution to that problem, or suddenly sees the hidden connection.
>
> DfEE/QCA (1999 : 14)

So there is a clear intention to acknowledge the creativity in mathematics. One issue that is important is how the creativity in mathematics might compare with other subjects and this may be mathematics' biggest problem. Creativity in other subjects is colourful, showy and clearly lots of fun; it doesn't look like work. It immediately appears accessible by all; I don't need to be able to draw to create my own pictures, I could be taking pictures with a digital camera, for example. The creativity seen in the public domain from mathematics comes from the earth-shattering category like proving of Fermat's last theorem by Andrew Wiles (Singh 1997), for example. This doesn't feel anywhere near as accessible as the creativity in art. How can we solve mathematics' image problem? Maybe one way of looking at creativity in mathematics is not to compare it with other subjects and not to expect the same from mathematics as other subjects, particularly the arts.

A 'new look' for creative mathematics

If creative mathematics is not to be viewed as the same as creativity in other subjects, how could this creativity be constructed? What might our expectation be? What can mathematics offer to the creativity debate? The following are some thoughts about how we might proceed with a new perspective for creativity in teaching and learning mathematics:

- Creativity in mathematics is different from creativity in other subjects.
- Creativity in mathematics is not about new solutions, for when children arrive at a known solution to a problem it is as creative as finding a new answer.
- Children can arrive at creativity ways of working but they need to be generalisable in order that children's own methods do not result in misconceptions.
- Creativity can support success in mathematics and therefore lessen children's anxieties about mathematics.
- When children are working on mathematics we need to recognise that all learning involves creativity if children are constructing their own meanings from activities.

- Creativity in mathematics is not just about specific resources and/or activities but about the process as well within learning mathematics.
- Creativity is more likely to occur when activities are resourced with high quality materials.
- Creativity in mathematics is not limited to problem solving.
- Creativity in mathematics involves high levels of cognitive challenge.
- All those working with children need to be aware that creativity is possible within mathematics and actively look for evidence of its occurrence.
- All those working with children should have opportunities to experience creativity within mathematics so they are better able to facilitate this for children.
- All those working with children should be making connections within mathematics explicit for children to facilitate creativity within mathematics.
- Creativity is more likely to occur in mathematics through skilful questioning of children as they work.
- Creativity can occur through an emphasis on reflecting on the process of undertaking mathematics whether that be in oral and/or written form.
- Creativity teaching of mathematics is possible across the Early Years and Primary age range without using worksheets.

Task

Reread the bullet points of the 'new look' creativity for mathematics. Are there any points here that you do not agree with? Which might you wish to change? How do these match your current teaching situation? What might you want to change in your teaching that would allow for more of these to happen?

In this chapter the nature of mathematics has been briefly explored and how this links to notions of creativity. The perceptions of mathematics as a subject have had a negative effect on the degree to which creativity is thought to be possible in mathematics. It also explores some of the problems of creativity in relation to generalisable rules and procedures. The chapter ends with a suggested 'new look' for thinking about creativity in mathematics and arguing that mathematics should be seen as different from other subjects. The following chapters in this book explore how the 'new look' for mathematics may be developed.

CHAPTER 2

Curriculum constraints and possibilities

In this chapter the focus is on the place of learning and teaching mathematics within the current curricular context in the UK. It will explore the constraints of the curriculum and some of the possibilities that the curriculum offers for developing creative learning and teaching of mathematics.

At the time of writing this book, the climate for Primary-aged learners has altered from a specific focus just on the daily numeracy lesson for Primary children to a clear consideration of the cross-curricular nature of learning and teaching. Although the topic approach was previously heavily criticised, specifically in relation to the tokenism that occurred for some subjects and the lack of coherent planning of progression in learning, this approach has resurfaced. With the introduction of Excellence and Enjoyment, numeracy across the curriculum was back on the agenda. The emphasis here, though, is about using mathematical skills within other subjects, for example drawing and interpreting graphs within science. So although the shift in emphasis appears to offer more freedoms there are still clear expectations of the specific skills to be acquired by the learners.

In 2008, the Early Years with the Foundation Stage guidance current for 3–5 will become the Early Years Foundation Stage from 0–5, incorporating the birth to three with the 3–5 guidance. This guidance has play at the heart of the approach to learning which allows for exploration, imagination and innovation from both learners and the adults who work with them. The guidance appears to offer both learners and their adults more flexibility yet Ofsted (2007) highlighted that although there were opportunities for children to develop their creativity in relation to mathematics the focus was the lack of opportunities for achievement with calculations. Within the current consultations for the new EYFS there is a proposed strand of 'problem solving, reasoning and numeracy'. This area of Learning and Development suggests that practitioners must support children in developing their understanding of problem solving, reasoning and numeracy in a broad range of contexts in which they can explore, enjoy, learn, practise and talk about their developing understanding. Practitioners must also offer opportunities for these skills to be practised, in order to give children confidence and competence in their use. After consultation there may be alterations to this guidance before the implementation in 2008.

Currently this area of Learning and Development is intended to include seeking patterns, making connections, recognising relationships, working with numbers, shapes, space and measures, and counting, sorting and matching. Children use their knowledge and skills in these areas to solve problems, generate new questions and make connections across other areas of Learning and Development.

The guidance for how this mathematical understanding should be developed is through stories, songs, games and imaginative play. The following give the practitioners possibilites to explore how they will offer children the best opportunities for effective mathematical development:

- many different activities, some of which will focus on mathematical development and some of which will draw out the mathematical learning in other activities, including observing numbers and patterns in the environment and in daily routines

- practical activities underpinned by children's developing communication skills

- activities that are imaginative and enjoyable

- real-life problems, for example: 'How many spoons do we need for everyone in this group to have one?'

- modelling mathematical vocabulary during the daily routines and throughout practitioner-led activities

- giving children sufficient time, space and encouragement to use 'new' words and mathematical ideas, concepts and language during child-initiated activities in their own play

- encouraging children to explore problems, to make patterns and to count and match together

- the balance between learning and teaching indoors and outdoors (e.g. having read a story about washing clothes, there might be laundrette play indoors and washing line play outdoors; streets of clothes shops built out of recyclables; bikes and other wheeled vehicles being used as delivery vans; numbered and lettered parking spaces. The practioners would spend time in both environments and the level of child-initiated and practitioner-led activity would be monitored and divided more or less equally across both environments. Displays would include examples from both environments.) For more details about the discussion of the use of displays see Chapter 9.

- help for those children who use a means of communication other than spoken English in developing and understanding specific mathematical language

- opportunities to observe, assess and plan the next stage in children's learning
- relevant training to improve practitioners' knowledge, skills and understanding.
(www.standards.dfes.gov.uk/primaryframeworks/foundation/psrn/)

This guidance has had an impact on the teaching and learning in y1 and y2 as the children move towards the National Curriculum. The transition between the curricular has enabled a freeing up of the teaching style in KS1. This is an important shift, as in 2000 Ofsted were reporting that schools should 'ensure that pupils have sufficient experience of full literacy hours and daily mathematics lessons before they enter Y1' as part of an HMI survey of the teaching of literacy and numeracy in reception classes. The emphasis on the style of learning and teaching was coming from the strategy towards the Foundation stage. The impact is now going in the reverse direction partly showing more of an awareness of the need for clear transition arrangements for children ensuring progress in their learning and their experiences.

For Primary-aged learners the new Strategy guidance includes amended learning objectives from the original strategy materials. A clearer structure for teaching mathematics has been provided by simplifying the structure of the objectives. The seven strands of learning give a broad overview of the mathematics curriculum in the Primary phase. Objectives are aligned to the seven strands to demonstrate progression in each strand.

The seven strands are not equally weighted. In constructing the strands, knowledge of number facts has been separated from calculation, methods of calculation have been unified, measures have been kept separate from shape and space, and problem solving has been embedded into the broader strand of using and applying mathematics. The seven strands relate very readily to the 1999 Framework and the programmes of study in the National Curriculum Orders for mathematics. Covering the objectives in the seven strands will support children in their progression towards the Early Learning Goals and the appropriate National Curriculum levels at KS1 and KS2.

The seven strands are as follows:

- using and applying mathematics
- counting and understanding number
- knowing and using number facts
- calculating
- understanding shape
- measuring
- handling data.

The construction of the mathematics Framework around seven strands not only simplifies the overall structure, but highlights the important areas of mathematics children need to learn to make effective progress.

> ### Task
>
> It is worth revisiting the curriculum documentation and guidance that you use and reading the introductory sections again. The intentions set out in these sections can become overlooked with continual use as the focus of our attention becomes how to translate the curriculum into action. What do you notice on rereading this material? Are there any surprises about the expectations identified in this material?

This structure could appear quite constrained and when the strategy was first introduced one of the foci was the structure of the three-part lesson with a mental oral starter, a main activity and a plenary. The latter is now referred to as a review of the lesson. This structure was a support for those teaching mathematics but it was also a constraint as teachers felt they had to stick to this structure for every lesson with no deviations, especially as Ofsted appeared to be looking for this in all of their observations. In the last review the focus was quite different and they were looking for cross-curricular working . . . 'but very few were successfully planning for the development of mathematics across the curriculum.' (Ofsted 2006)

The National Numeracy Framework is the other curriculum document that has both supported teachers but also acted as a constraint to practice. It has supported teachers because it had a clear structure linked to year groups and expected outcomes against the National Curriculum. It has constrained initial thinking because it offered a pattern of areas to be covered for each term within the year group. Martin Hughes (1999: 4) described the numeracy strategy as '. . . undoubtedly the most prescriptive approach to primary mathematics ever developed in this country.' Teachers felt the pressure to 'cover' the content of each term regardless of the successes or difficulties of the learners, the message appeared to be about keeping the pace of teaching going, not just in individual lessons but also in relation to the topic areas covered. This created dilemmas for teachers who knew that some children had not succeeded with topics and yet there was a pressure to move on.

Although the Numeracy Strategy and the National Curriculum outlined a range of aspects of mathematics to be taught and learnt, the focus was clearly about emphasising calculation skills and knowledge. Hughes (1999) describes '. . . the key objectives listed for each year group (as) almost entirely concerned with number knowledge and calculation, with relatively little attention to problem solving.' This had a significant impact on the teaching and learning of mathematics and began with guidance in the Numeracy project of three days lessons on numeracy and two days on other areas of the mathematics curriculum each week. The other thing that the emphasis on numeracy and a daily lesson encouraged was a separation of mathematics from the rest of the curriculum. This was despite the guidance given from the Department of Education.

[handwritten: Play would allow for integration of subjects]

> Remember that the purpose of the daily mathematics lesson is not to fulfil a rigidly-defined routine but to teach mathematics well.
>
> (DfEE 1999: 16)

As mathematics was given up to an hour a day (depending upon age group) this created pressure on the space left for other subjects. The result of this was again initially less integration of mathematics with the rest of the subjects taught. Mathematics was already getting a large proportion of the time allocated and other subject areas were losing status and ground in the time allotted for teaching. The other issue that arose for schools was the potentially wide ability range being taught in many classes. Larger schools went over to setting for numeracy and literacy and sometimes this was from Y1 right through the school. This added to the separation from the rest of the curriculum as a class could be set into different classes in the morning but in mixed ability groups combining different experiences from the morning into the rest of the curriculum in the afternoon. All these factors increased the separation of mathematics teaching and learning from the rest of the curriculum. Teachers could not make connections between mathematics lessons content from the morning to other activities in the afternoon particularly when they may not have a clear idea about what had actually occurred in the lessons. Teachers with children from their classes in several different sets do not have the same information about the teaching and learning they are not part of. Records can help but they cannot give you the same insights into children's thinking. This also works in the other direction as teachers may not be able to make the connections from other activities across the curriculum into mathematics. Why is this important to make connections for children? Research work conducted at King's College and funded by the TDA illustrates the importance for teacher effectiveness.

Askew, Brown, Rhodes, Wiliam and Johnson (1997) identified different teacher orientations and their effectiveness in teaching numeracy.

Transmission

The teachers with this orientation emphasise the role of the teacher as the source of mathematical knowledge and they impart the knowledge to pupils focusing on mathematics as a discrete set of rules and procedures. The children's role is subordinate to the teacher and they are the receivers of the knowledge. This may feel a familiar approach to thinking about teaching and learning if you have considered behaviourist views previously.

Discovery

Teachers with this orientation emphasise the children at the centre of the learning process where the child constructs or discovers mathematical ideas for themselves. The teacher is the provider of activities, resources and support for the children's discoveries. Mathematics is not seen as purely rules and procedures. The links here are with constructivist approaches to teaching and learning. Discovery replaces the telling children advocated in the transmission orientation. The support is the scaffolding of children's learning.

Connectionist

Teachers with this orientation emphasise the work on the complexity of mathematics – children and teachers together. In the lessons observed as part of the study they shared their own strategies for doing mathematics with children. The teacher is not seen as the only source of mathematical knowledge. They value children's methods and explanation. They importantly establish connections within the mathematics curriculum. A simple example is the link between addition and multiplication. These teachers were also considered to be the most effective in terms of learning in relation to test outcomes. This orientation is considered to be the closest to the apprenticeship model of teaching and learning of which you may be aware. It is associated with Rogoff and Lave (1984) who focused on learning in very different environments than classrooms and often with older learners.

> **Task**
>
> How do you see your teaching orientated? Are you more of a transmission, a discovery or a connectionist teacher?

The Primary National Strategy

With the shift to the Primary National Strategy covering the Foundation stage and KS1 and KS2 the focus of attention has also shifted from teaching to learning. In the Excellence and Enjoyment materials (2004) the Learning to Learn section defines aspects of learning. The following are the selection of those most applicable to mathematics:

- *Enquiry*
  These skills enable children to ask relevant questions, to pose and define problems, to plan what to do and how to research, to predict outcomes and anticipate responses, to test conclusions and improve ideas (adapted from the National Curriculum 2000).

- *Problem solving*

  The key skill of problem solving involves children in developing the skills and strategies that will help them to solve problems they face in learning and in life. Problem solving includes the skills of identifying and understanding the problems, planning ways to solve the problem, monitoring progress in tackling a problem and reviewing a solution to a problem (adapted from the National Curriculum 2000).

- *Creative thinking*

  These skills enable children to generate and extend ideas, to suggest hypotheses, to apply imagination, and to look for alternative innovative outcomes (adapted from the National Curriculum 2000).

- *Information processing*

  These skills enable children to locate and collect relevant information, to sort, classify, sequence, compare, contrast, and to analyse part/whole relationships (adapted from the National Curriculum 2000).

- *Reasoning*

  These skills enable children to give reasons for opinions and actions, to draw inferences and make deductions, to use precise language to explain what they think, and to make judgements and decisions informed by reasons or evidence (adapted from the National Curriculum 2000).

- *Evaluation*

  These skills enable children to evaluate information, to judge the value of what they read, hear or do, to develop criteria for judging the value of their own and others' work or ideas, and to have confidence in their judgements (adapted from the National Curriculum 2000).

- *Communication*

  The key skill of communication includes skills in speaking, listening, reading and writing. Skills in speaking and listening include the ability to speak effectively for different audiences; to listen, understand and respond appropriately to others; and to participate effectively in group discussion. Skills in reading and writing include the ability to read fluently a range of . . . (texts) . . . and reflect critically on what is read; and the ability to write fluently for a range of purposes and audiences . . . (adapted from the National Curriculum 2000).

There are possibilities in each of these areas for a creative approach to learning and teaching mathematics across the age range. In order to show how these aspects can connect to mathematics learning and teaching and a creative approach, the following begins to bring these together and offer a small number of activities in mathematics.

Enquiry

Skills

To ask relevant questions; to pose and define problems; to plan what to do and how to research; to predict outcomes and anticipate responses; and to test conclusions and improve ideas.

Activities in mathematics

Activities that begin with a practical starting point offer opportunities for children to talk about the questions, refine the tasks and plan responses including problem solving, investigations and word problems.

Problem solving

Skills

Developing the skills and strategies that will help them to solve problems they face in learning and in life; skills of identifying and understanding the problems, planning ways to solve the problem; and monitoring progress in tackling a problem and reviewing a solution to a problem.

Activities in mathematics

These skills can be developed through activities which include investigations, problem solving, real-life problem solving and word problems. Monitoring progress for complex problems and investigations can be completed through journaling or writing reviews of the processes.

Creative thinking

Skills

To generate and extend ideas; to suggest hypotheses; to apply imagination; and to look for alternative innovative outcomes.

Activities in mathematics

These skills can be developed through designing games, questions for others to answer, looking for solutions to historical problems and real-life problems. They could also be developed through mathematics trails and links with trips focusing on mathematics.

Information processing

Skills

To locate and collect relevant information; to sort, classify, sequence, compare, contrast; and to analyse part/whole relationships.

Activities in mathematics

Using data from historical sources would give children the opportunities to explore the relationships between information given and events that took place. Reflective journaling would give children the opportunity to analyse the part/whole relationships.

Reasoning

Skills

To give reasons for opinions and actions, to draw inferences and make deductions; to use precise language to explain what they think; and to make judgements and decisions informed by reasons or evidence.

Activities in mathematics

Opportunities will be created to develop reasoning skills through any activity that promotes discussion and written responses.

Evaluation

Skills

To evaluate information; to judge the value of what they read, hear or do; to develop criteria for judging the value of their own and others' work or ideas; and to have confidence in their judgements.

Activities in mathematics

Evaluating different methods for calculating and when it is most appropriate to use them will give opportunities for children to make judgements. Historical and geographical data that is used to evaluate actions will offer opportunities to judge the value of others' work, as would peer-assessment and feedback. Evaluating their own and others' work through self- and peer assessment and through the process of journaling.

Communication

Skills

To speak effectively for different audiences; to listen, understand and respond appropriately to others; to participate effectively in group discussion; to read fluently a range of . . . (texts) . . . and reflect critically on what is read; and to write fluently for a range of purposes and audiences.

Activities in mathematics

Again, any activity that promotes the need for discussion and recording will assist in the development of these skills. Word problems will emphasise reading, as will using data from historical and geographical sources. Journaling and written explanations will offer opportunities for written communication for a range of audiences.

> **Task**
>
> Think about the range of activities given to the children over the last week. Which of those gave children opportunities to develop the aspects of learning – enquiry, problem solving, creative thinking, information processing, reasoning, evaluation or communication?

The creativity strand comes through aspects of the National Curriculum documentation and guidance though not explicitly always in mathematical development and mathematics. Creativity has become a key focus of policy and therefore the development of practice though the shift is that creativity is across the curriculum and not a province of the arts alone. The National Curriculum in action produced QCA materials entitled *Creativity: find it, promote it* which included a range of examples of creative practice across the curriculum and across the age range. What this did not do, however, was to acknowledge the constraints and challenges of teachers developing creativity in education. The mathematics example offered on the website is 'Tasty maths' for Y9 which unfortunately does not offer any support for the creative development of teaching mathematics earlier in the education system. It is worth looking at the conception of creative teaching here from an Early Years and Primary perspective. The changes to practice here, you may feel, are no different to 'good practice'. Although not a very innovative example it should give others confidence that they can teach creatively and maybe do things better.

Part of the attention to creativity is the links with technological innovation, celebrating what is done well and a concern about the UK being left behind. This was echoed in *The Roberts' Report, Nurturing Creativity in Young People*, published in July 2006, which offers a framework for the development of creativity from the Early Years, through mainstream education and other settings, leading eventually to pathways into the Creative Industries. For the Roberts' report creative thinking and behaviour encourage children's personal learning and thinking skills. These the report sees as underpinning children becoming successful and independent learners. Creativity is also seen as a way of engaging those who have become disaffected with education and what it has to offer them and their futures. This approach can offer a fresh challenge to those settings and schools who have become successful against the current attainment measures and the report suggests it can also help those settings and schools in challenging situations. There appears to be a realisation that some of the teaching and learning strategies have failed to enthuse and motivate our young people. Concerns about accountability have narrowed the flexibility and creativity in teaching. We have focused on the teaching and perhaps assumed that the learning would follow as a matter of course. Learning has become the main focus whilst not ignoring teaching. Creative children need creative teachers.

Linked with the personalised learning agenda, this creates challenges for teachers and adults working with children to planning appropriate curricula so that every child can achieve their potential.

This is brought together to focus on the barriers to children and young people's learning in Every Child Matters (ECM). Table 2.1 links ECM with creativity and particularly creative approaches to teaching and learning mathematics.

Table 2.1 Every Child Matters and creative mathematics teaching and learning *appendix*

Outcomes	Approaches to mathematics including skills and knowledge
Be Healthy	Creative approaches to learning and teaching mathematics can improve children's self-esteem and confidence with successes in mathematics and this contributes to children's emotional well-being. It reduces mathematics anxiety through attention to the affective domain.
Stay Safe	Increasing group work can help children to negotiate appropriately and develop relationships. Role-play in mathematics can assist this development.
Enjoy and Achieve	Developing critical, logical thinking and problem solving skills. This includes word problems, investigations and real-life problem solving. Creative approaches to teaching and learning mathematics can support increases in achievement and a decrease in mathematics anxiety.
Make a Positive Contribution	Skills developed including an understanding of how mathematics and particularly data affects our daily lives.
Achieve Economic Well-being	Creativity is a key employability skill within a whole range of industries. Understanding the use of data and monetary skills can support economic wellbeing.

Task

Look at your institution's development plan and the relationship with the five ECM outcomes. What items might you be able to pick out as having a direct effect on the developments of mathematics learning and teaching?

This chapter has explored the curriculum constraints but also the changing current climete which refocuses learning at the centre of education. This shift provides opportunities for creative thinking about the learning and teaching of mathematics and the links with the themes for development from the Primary National Strategy (PNS) and other policy documentation like Every Child Matters. Suggestions on further future development will be discussed in the final chapter, 'The sky's the limit'.

Starting points for creative teaching

This chapter looks at how to begin the process of teaching mathematics creatively. It explores whether or not this is possible. Woods (1995) researched creative teachers in the Primary school and in his introduction cited Waller (1932) who believed that teaching led teachers to become people of routine and as a result of their role not a creative profession. Interestingly, Woods does not support this stance but found through his research certain creative qualities in abundance. He identified four major components of creative teachers, innovation, ownership, control and relevance. Teachers innovate their practice developing their own ideas, situations or maybe adapting others' starting points. Creative teachers take ownership of the teaching they have planned and taught. This involves taking the extensive guidance from the National Curriculum, Numeracy Strategy and associated materials and making them their own, adapting them to fit the needs of their learners and enabling the learners to engage with the subject matter. It also involves making the links with the agendas of personalised learning and the breaking down of barriers to learning from ECM. The other side of the ownership is handing over the ownership of the learning to the learners and allowing them to take a path which the teacher may not have originally intended. Early Years practitioners are particularly good at working in this way, going with the interests of the child. Over the years Primary teachers have lost some of the confidence required to allow this to happen in lessons, with the pressures of coverage of the curriculum, assessment results and inspection regimes. Now with the Primary National Strategy and a focus on personalised learning the time is ripe for a review of the control of teaching and learning. Clearly ownership links with control and teachers have felt they have had limited control over the content and methods of teaching mathematics since the introduction of the Numeracy Strategy. Again the timing is right to review the locus of control particularly if the needs of the children are paramount. The last area of relevance is a very important one for mathematics as society's view of mathematics is that although it is a utilitarian subject the amount of mathematics you use in everyday life is limited. Mathematics needs to be made relevant to the children through making connections with its use in different contexts and again the cross-curricular links emphasised in the PNS assist teachers in adapting the teaching and learning that takes place.

We believe it is possible to begin to teach mathematics creatively even if you don't feel that you are creative. We first explore some of the obstacles that exist and then we look at some simple ways of thinking about teaching including the environment which can change classroom practice. The first set of suggestions is intended to give ideas of starting points that will encourage you to consider other ideas to incorporate into your teaching. We will then focus on being creative in response to situations that arise in the classroom.

What are the main obstacles in the cultivation of creativity in the practice of mathematical education in the Primary and Early Years?

There is an environment of conformity in the classroom when mathematics is being taught. It is completed in specific ways. The National Numeracy Strategy has had a large impact on the format of lessons taught and the emphasis on specific styles of teaching since its introduction. If we couple this with the Ofsted inspections which have focused on the implementation of the strategies, teachers have found it hard to justify moving away from the formats suggested. This area is also a very delicate social problem connected with the tradition of school practice and the social expectations of learning mathematics. The focus is clearly on basic arithmetic skills that will be needed for future life.

There is a large amount of formal knowledge to be learned in the mathematics curriculum and therefore there can be concerns about covering the curriculum content. To move away from the content or even not have control over what might be learnt, again linked to accountability, means teachers understandably playing safe.

The initial training of new teachers has again concentrated on implementation of strategies and, in the case of mathematics, the three-part lesson. Teachers have had more guidance on how and what to teach in mathematics through the strategy materials than ever before. Training establishments have also been inspected to see if they are producing teachers who are able to teach mathematics independently through the implementation of the strategy materials. Teachers have not been prepared for the creative work with children according to their own formal education and then the requirements of the standards for QTS in their training.

With the introduction of the Primary Strategy and creativity as a focus of the curriculum, and the pedagogy right across the Early Years and Primary, the balance is being readdressed. It is acceptable to adapt the guidance to meet the needs and the learning styles of the children. For mathematics this means a relaxation of the adherence to the three-part lesson and integration of mathematics with other subjects. For some teachers this may feel like a return to where they have been before; the topic approach. What is clear is that this is not an attempt to reinstate that approach as a whole but to look carefully at the way knowledge, skills and learning cross the boundaries of subject domains. The research of Jeffrey and Woods (2003) into creative teaching suggests that teachers feel creative when they control taking ownership of their practice. The current changes to the curriculum guidance are giving back to teachers some of that ownership. They can, as Jeffrey and Woods (2003) indicate, innovate ensuring that learning is relevant to the children they teach through exploring different ways of working.

> **Task**
>
> How do you work with the NNS and all the guidance materials? How far do you feel you can adapt the materials presented? Are you empowered by colleagues to adapt to meet the needs of your learners?

How can you cultivate the creativity in the classroom?

A starting point for creative teaching can be difficult to identify if you don't see yourself as being a creative person. Part of the problem with this view arises from thinking that the creative approach has to be a large change to teaching and involve a large number of resources. The truth is that a creative approach can come from small changes to existing practice. A very creative teacher – training student altered the start of a lesson by putting on a white coat and introducing herself as a scientist. She altered the date on the board to the future and the scenario for a specific situation began to unfold for the class. Perhaps the biggest change here is the confidence of the teacher to try something different and to take a risk. This can be the most difficult part of the process. It is easy to stay with tried and trusted approaches as they work and the teacher is in control of the situation. In changing the approach the teacher changes the rules and also the potential responses of the children. The situation is not totally in their control, there are risks and this requires confidence from the teacher. If I don't know what the potential outcomes are, how can I feel able to answer children's questions, for example? The children may be working in different ways which may require establishing different ground rules for behaviour.

> **Task**
>
> Think about the teachers that you consider are creative, how do they take risks with their teaching? What do they alter? How do they manage the control issues or the feelings of lack of control over where their teaching will take the children? You may not see creative teaching in mathematics but that doesn't matter to begin with, what you are looking for are the skills and approaches regardless of the subject taught.

Mathematics may feel like a subject without the scope for creativity. It is possible to use ideas from other areas of the curriculum to develop the creative teaching in mathematics. Teachers who are very confident with their teaching of another subject area may be more creative in that area than mathematics. Sometimes it can be hard to transfer the skills and approaches in one subject to another yet we can learn from others and our own strengths in another area as the following shows.

Ideas for creative teaching from developments in other areas of the curriculum

Just because it is not directly related to mathematics doesn't mean the ideas for teaching are not helpful in being creative about the approach taken. In teaching mathematics we can learn from creative ideas developed within other curriculum areas and adapt them to support the teaching and learning. A good idea is one that can be adapted for teaching purposes across the curriculum and across the age range. An example of this might be to take the science suggestion from above when working on imperial measures. Dress up in some 'old' clothes and turn the clock back, as it were. Change the date on the board to 1966, put the desks in rows and then teach the rough equivalents of imperial measures to metric units.

Write dance

An interesting idea from English, Write Dance by Oussoren (2000), is another example. It is a handwriting methodology for children throughout the Primary school years developed in the 1980s by Ragnhild Oussoren Voors, a consultant graphologist. It was originally based on the writing psychology from France in the late nineteenth century. The originator has very successfully developed her approach to the teaching of writing in most Scandinavian countries as well as Germany, France and Holland. Since the late 1990s it has become used increasingly in the UK. It teaches writing through tapping into the emotions and natural movements of children. Write Dance is a combination of physical activity and making marks on paper. It is designed to develop children's coordination skills in order to promote a personal, rhythmic, fluent and legible style of handwriting. It seeks to make this connection through a series of sessions that combine a response to music, large body movements and the development of fine motor coordination.

Write Dance allows children to learn all the skills in a fun and non-threatening way. Each of the themes in the materials is designed to develop a specific movement. The children usually begin by practising specific large movements and once the movements have been mastered, the music begins and everyone moves to the beat or in response to the music depending on the theme. The children use different materials to make the movements on a writing surface. This may be anything from crayons on paper to washing-up liquid on a plastic mat. Over time, these movements on the surface become smaller and smaller as the children gain control and confidence to explore, enjoy and have fun.

A visit to a Y2 class in a school where the approach was being used saw the children listening to music, lying on the floor with their eyes shut and making the movements with arms and legs, to support the movements needed for writing different shapes connected to the movements they will repeat for handwriting. After a concentrated period of listening and moving, where they draw the shapes in the air, they get up and repeat the movements on paper using both hands and arms. The same process can be undertaken for writing numbers and shapes. This approach supports the visual and kinaesthetic learners and has the added bonus for mathematical development in that it also encourages the children's visualisation, which will support later learning of geometrical ideas.

> ### Task
> What innovations are happening in other curriculum areas? Could some of the key ideas be adapted to support the teaching and learning of mathematics?

Resources

Resources for creative approaches to teaching are very important, as the quality of the resources will allow children as well as the teachers to adapt ideas. These do not have to be expensive resources but can start with collections of shapes, dice, odd sample tiles, carpet squares, bags and other containers. The more accessible and wide ranging the resources the more potential for children to use these to bring their creative thinking to mathematics.

Number sacks

The same is true of the kinds of resources available for teaching mathematics creatively. In the Early Years many classrooms have story sacks, which contain a book, soft toys of the characters from the story and games or other associated activities. The same kind of resources can be made for children to explore aspects of mathematics. For example, a number sack or a sack/box of items can be put together to focus attention on a mathematical idea like odd and even. In this case the stimulus is looking at ladybirds, with a large ladybird on card and spots to place on each side of the back of the ladybird to make even and/or odd numbers of spots. A soft toy or puppet ladybird and a suitable book about ladybirds and/or odd and even numbers all combine to focus items on odd and even for children to explore as part of free-play situations or as resources for teaching the class or groups about the mathematical ideas.

Obviously some stories have a clear focus on a specific number. *Goldilocks and the Three Bears* could be a sack with three bowls, three chairs, three bears and three beds to emphasise 'threeness'. A sack focusing on triangles might include: a small book about triangles, a tetrahedron, several 2-D triangles, a pin board and some elastic bands, and a template for drawing triangles.

Boxes or suitcases

Although the focus starts with Early Years, the collections idea can be adapted for teaching older Primary children. A box of a collection of money from another country, some maps and a bill from some items purchased in the country could be the starting point for an investigation into exchange rates and exploration on the internet about the country's money system and the relationship between the coins and notes in the money system.

With the introduction of the Primary Strategy and the return to thematic or topic areas, the need to develop teaching activities which allow children to explore several curriculum areas at once have come back into schools. So the idea of the money from another country in a box might be extended to include maps, postcards and other information to support an exploration of the country more generally. Or a box might contain travel information from which the children have to find out where the person has travelled to and how long it has taken them from the information given in the box. This might include:

- a bus or train timetable
- an airline ticket
- a receipt for coffee at an airport/station with date and time
- a postcard
- some money
- a ticket for an event or access to visit a landmark
- possibly some instructions for a task for a group/individual to complete.

The information may be placed in a small or old suitcase to give the feel of a journey or the sense of travel to add to the overall feel of the activity. Again, the advantage of this approach is that the resources can be altered/updated for different groups of children and used more than once. Differentiation can be supported by the variety of contents, the task set and/or the support given to complete the task. This makes a clear difference from a worksheet on train timetables for a Y6 class, adding interest and variety. The children get to handle objects, there is a reason for a group to discuss potential approaches to gaining the necessary information to complete the task and, if asked to give a report of their findings, a clear reason for needing to record the outcomes of the task.

> **Task**
>
> Can you think of a resource like the ones outlined previously that you have/could use with your learners? If you haven't tried an idea like this, have a go. Talk to a colleague about your ideas and the children's responses.

If we look carefully at the approaches being taken to developing creative practice in the Early Years we can see some specific ideas that can be linked directly to the teaching and learning of mathematics. The following from Tina Bruce's *Cultivating Creativity in Babies, Toddlers and Young Children* is just such an example:

> *. . . being offered a wide range of materials through which to express creative ideas . . .*
>
> *Organising a learning environment which provokes . . .*
>
> (Bruce 2004: 93)

For children to be creative they need to be able to explore materials within a stimulating learning environment. This is not just in the confines of the buildings but also the outdoor environment. The focus on the outdoors in the Foundation stage has resulted in a number of developments of school grounds for teaching and learning in the Early Years. From these developments what can KS2, for example, take that would support mathematics teaching and learning? Could Y6 design activities for the younger children to enhance mathematics in the outdoors?

> **Task**
>
> What kind of outdoor environment does your school/setting have? What kinds of resources are available for children to explore mathematics in nature in this space? Can they use mathematical equipment outside and not just on fine days?

Is this problem solving?

One difficulty that is often encountered with looking at different resources and approaches to teaching mathematics is the link or not with problem solving. As soon as there is a mention of cross-curricular work or rethinking mathematics teaching it is assumed that this is problem solving. Problem solving is commonly used as a cross-curricular approach with mathematics. Coles and Copeland (2002) and Turner and McCullouch (2004) both use problem solving as their starting point for cross-curricular links. Coles and Copeland were influenced by their involvement in Open University courses, which directly focused on problem solving as key mathematical skills. This approach is about developing the children's abilities to use and apply mathematical knowledge. This may not be introduced to children in a creative way. In fact, one of the criticisms of the problem solving movement was that teachers began to teach problem solving rubrics; they were teaching a method which the children then followed every time they encountered a 'problem to solve'. As a consequence, the richness of 'real problem solving' situations where children could explore the context, data and then begin to make the problem their own faded from classrooms.

'Real life' problem solving for the NNS is exemplified by a Y3 one-step problem: 'A spider has 8 legs. How many legs do 5 spiders have? Now work out how many legs 6 spiders have.' This is an example of a one-step word problem, which is placed in a so-called 'real life' context to add interest. This is not the same as creating opportunities for children to explore mathematics creatively or for teachers to teach mathematics creatively. In the context of teaching, therefore, we are not using teaching creatively to mean teaching problem solving. Problem solving is also used as a term to indicate that the problems are actually word problems, to be solved with a given solution. All these have one outcome and usually the numbers and any other measurements involved are neat and easy to work with. Real life problem solving is messy; the numbers are not easy whether they are actually numbers or measures. There is not necessarily only one answer but there can be several potential answers to the problem. What makes them real problems? A real problem is a problem only when the person solving the problem considers it a real problem to be solved. Our concentration in this chapter is thinking about making the teaching more interesting for the learners and stimulating enquiry.

The following example of a starting point for teaching could be seen as a problem to solve or we would suggest that it offers a way of getting children to think about mathematics differently. We could teach the shoe question detailed in the following section as a problem and get the children to use a problem-solving rubric but that would not allow them to bring their own ideas to the situation. We want children to be able to use and apply their knowledge but flexibly.

Scaled objects
Objects of a different scale can be an interesting starting point for different age groups. A large shoe, for example, can lead to a question being posed about the shoe size of the large shoe. If we assume that there is a relationship between the length of the shoe and the size of the shoe we are able to work out the shoe size of any given shoe. This activity involved the children in measuring, comparing and calculating. Large or small items can be used to produce the equivalent scale for objects given, so for a large cup how big would the saucer be? Or what size would the spoon need

to be? For a small doll representing a child how big would a stool be for the child to sit on?

Task

Using an example like the shoe, think about what you would need to do to encourage children to begin work on the situation. Could they pose their own questions from the situation set up by you? What skills and knowledge might they need to be able to engage with the situation? How would you manage this kind of task in the classroom?

Puzzle and logic

Another starting point can be a puzzle to solve. An example of this is the following although this is not actually a real problem. A race has five runners. Bets are placed on the outcomes of the race. To place a bet you must bet on two propositions, and you will win only if you are wholly successful, that is both your propositions come true. At the end of the race three bettors lost these bets:

---

1   A will not win the gold, or B the silver.

2   C will win a medal, and D will not.

3   D and E will both win medals.

4   D will not win the silver, or E the bronze.

5   A will win a medal, and C will not.

Who won which of the medals? (Answer: A wins gold, D wins silver and C bronze)

The object behind these kinds of puzzles is to encourage logic thinking, moving from what is known to what is not known.

Task

Look for a logic puzzle or problem to try with children that will allow children to begin to develop their logical thinking.

Using different teaching strategies

Sometimes, in order to make the teaching creative, it is not the subject content that is the starting point but the teaching and learning strategies that are employed in the lesson or session that are the source of the creative approach.

Learning tables or any other number bond can be seen as a simple yet unexciting aspect of teaching and learning mathematics. The following are a small range of approaches to this area that can be used in any lesson:

- A version of loop cards where children have one half of the number sentence and are asked to find the correct other half held by another member of the class.

- Large dominoes with an answer and a sentence on each half of the domino to match either as a class or a group activity to reinforce learning number facts by heart.

- Each child holds an answer and a multiplication table is on the board for two teams in a different order. The teams sit together and act as a relay team. The first child must identify where their answer goes on the board and attach the answer to the correct number sentence for their team before the next child may then do the same. The team continue to identify where each of the answers are placed until the whole team has completed the task. They are competing with the other teams to be the first one to complete the task.

- A small group of children are given the answers and they must make up the questions to go with the answers.

- A group are given a multiplication table and asked to look carefully at the table to write a set of strategies to help others to learn this set of facts. This will enable them to look closely at the patterns in the table and to share their own existing strategies within the group.

This chapter has tried to show the extent to which it is possible to creatively teach mathematics. It is not designed to give an exhaustive list of the ways this can be done but to offer a range of starting points to stimulate reflection upon current teaching practices and the potential to change. As Woods (1995) says: 'Creative teaching promotes creative learning' – something all teaching should aspire to.

The end of death by worksheet: being creative rather than using worksheets

Worksheets appear to be more commonplace in numeracy lessons than in any other area of the curriculum. All too frequently, both teachers and trainees teach wonderfully interactive whole class sessions but then resort to using differentiated worksheets or pages from mathematics schemes to provide the independent work. Indeed, the unit plans that many schools now use for their planning usually have the relevant worksheet/s attached. (www.standards.dfes.gov.uk/primary/features/mathematics/maths_unit_plans/)

Whilst there may be a time and a place for an occasional printed sheet to be used, with a little thought and creativity on the teacher's part a far more creative and rewarding experience can be provided for the children. One difficulty with worksheets is that they take away the opportunities for children to talk about mathematics and/or the opportunity to extend the questions asked. The questions in worksheets tend to be narrow and closed rather than open and collaborative tasks. The latter require extended written guidance to make them into independent work.

Why do teachers use worksheets?

One reason often given is that it saves time in preparing resources for a lesson or it fits into the school's scheme. The first can be countered as worksheets make assumptions about the level of work required by the child and this includes the level of reading required to access the activities. It takes time to read carefully through worksheets and consider the match between the work and the children within the class. Resources that are collected as an alternative to using a worksheet can be used time and time again whereas worksheets will always need copying for each lesson. The expected progression within worksheets can set the learners and the teachers specific difficulties within the lesson and rather than providing independent activities for a group can require greater adult intervention. Worksheets can be a good source of ideas but not necessarily presented in the exact format provided within the scheme or book chosen. Trainee teachers often see worksheets as a short cut but to use a worksheet effectively takes time to ensure that the worksheet is actually linked to the learning objectives of the lesson and the needs of the children in the classroom.

What are the problems that can occur with using worksheets?

Bennett and Desforges (1985) developed a typology for classroom tasks, consisting of task demands and chief characteristics:

- Incremental – introduce new ideas, procedures or skills; demands recognition, discrimination.
- Restructuring – demands the invention or discovery of an idea, process or pattern.
- Enrichment – demands application of familiar skills to new problems.
- Practice – demands the tuning of new skills on familiar problems.

One of the issues with worksheets is that they tend to focus on the practice skills and therefore do not always allow for the opportunity for children to have other demands placed upon them within the activity. These tasks are then seen as routine by the learners. Whether the task is novel or routine (Skemp 1979) determines the level of consciousness or amount of attention paid to it. The terms here can be seen as interchangeable. Routine activities can be completed with quite a low level of consciousness and therefore attention to the task itself. This seems to be another way of describing the overall level of attention to the task as the heightening of consciousness in activities brings about more accurate direction of behaviour, that is a focus of attention. Likewise, lowering the consciousness even within a seemingly routine task can result in ignoring a key element. An example of this type of response from children in relation to worksheets is when a child is filling in boxes on a sheet of questions assuming they involve addition only to find that the sheet is actually about subtraction. As a result a key element of the worksheet has been ignored; attention was needed to the symbols used throughout the sheet. Here the child immediately sees something familiar within the task and assumptions about the level of attention needed to complete the task. For children lacking confidence or those with a lower mathematical ability this may also affect their attitude to the task and influence their decisions about its level of difficulty.

Another example of how children's attention can shift within a worksheet activity is one involving the children in a reception class. A group were seated at a table with a worksheet in front of them which asked them to draw a number of fish in a net being pulled by a trawler. As the children's attention shifts from a focus on the numbers given on the sheet to the process of drawing the fish, decisions about whether or not the fish have eyes, fins or even bubbles emerging from their mouths become the important issues for the child, followed by whether they can colour them in or not. In terms of attention the focus is not on the mathematics for either the child drawing the small number of fish or the large number. What is the purpose behind this kind of task as far as the mathematics is concerned? One of the children interviewed did not make the connection between the activity of counting and being able to tell how many items she had. What will the children have taken away from this activity? So many similar activities can be found in worksheets.

A further example of a worksheet from a scheme asks the children to draw 20 dots after a series of pictures of objects to count followed by a box to write the number in. All these are under the headings of 'How many?', and 'Counting to 20'. Children appear to trust the adults and their choice of activities and so attempt to make sense of what is required. Children in fact become adept at focusing on the routines required to achieve the expected outcomes. An example of this was a child who was working in a workbook on a story of an 11 type activity. Within a caterpillar shape the child was given the start of the sequence of number sentences making 11, beginning with 10 + 1 = 11. When asked what he had to do the child said, 'That's easy – they all make 11 so you just write them in the boxes,' and proceeded to write the numbers in the appropriate boxes. Again, the question would be where was the child's attention whilst carrying out the task? If the child could spot the pattern so easily there are alternative ways of getting the child to look at the number of different ways of making 11 and how you could use the information to assist you with other problems, moving the children on from known facts to deriving facts from the known one.

Children even cope with more apparently obscure tasks not by making sense of the mathematics but by making sense of the routines within the activity. For example, a box on a worksheet with no contents visible but labelled 10 buns is followed by a picture of two buns. Underneath, the children are asked to complete, 'There are 10 buns and . . . buns. How many are there altogether?' There could be two reasonable answers given to the final question, 12 or 2. The latter because you can only see two buns in the picture, the rest are within the box. However children very quickly realise the rules of the activity and which numbers to place where, as the child with the caterpillar did, but what do they take away from the activity in terms of the mathematics?

Worksheets are not always clear for the learners, as can be seen from these examples. The children described here are looking for clues to help them make sense of the worksheets given to them as part of their mathematical experience. Is this the most helpful and effective approach to the teaching and their learning?

Task

Have a look at the worksheets you may have used most recently in your teaching. What is the learning purpose intended for the children completing these? How might you categorise the task in relation to Bennett and Desforges' typology offered earlier in the chapter? Where do you think the children's attention might be on the tasks given on the worksheet? Could there have been different ways of introducing the same task or could the whole focus of the task have been different? Were the worksheets just there for practise?

How do I make a choice of what to do that will move away from worksheets?

An alternative to starting with a worksheet is to look at a different starting point such as a practical task, which might be to simply throw two dice and calculate the total or the product. Then in order to evaluate whether or not the activity is really good it is possible to consider the following aspects of the task:

What makes a really 'good' activity?

- accessible for all
- possible to extend
- possible to narrow
- practical starting point
- offers opportunities for mathematical discussion
- offers a reason for children to record their ideas
- clarity of underlying mathematics
- offers opportunities for repetition without becoming meaningless – both for teachers and children!
- should be enjoyable!

(Briggs 2000)

As you read the rest of this chapter, use the list above to consider the tasks suggested and evaluate these in comparison to using a worksheet.

In the Early Years, worksheets can offer very stilted activities that would be much more interactive if the ideas behind the worksheet were translated into a practical activity. For example, a worksheet that asks children to sort shapes between two toys and place them on a plate in front of each toy is a very static task. The idea behind the activity is a sorting one and could be a practical sorting of shapes still between two toys but with the toys given an actual plate and shapes and toys. The activity changes completely from a 2-D worksheet to a 3-D task with real objects.

Task

Choose a worksheet and think about how you could present the same ideas to children but using a practical starting point rather than the sheet itself. You could try a worksheet with one group and a practical starting point to evaluate the differences between the tasks.

Graphical representation

Consider first the resources that are used for children to consolidate their understanding of graphical representations throughout the Early Years and Primary age range. After the initial flurry of pictograms and block charts to represent the eye colour of each class, or the children's favourite sandwich filling, all too frequently children don't see a purpose to either drawing or interpreting graphs. Why not link this work to science, for example growing beans? Plotting the weekly growth of each bean can soon lead to such questions as:

- When would you estimate your bean will reach 10 cm high?
- Does the bean grow at the same rate every week?
- What does the line joining your measured points indicate?
- Use your calculator to calculate how long it would take to grow 3 m, if it kept growing at the same rate as the first week.
- Looking at the way that growth eventually slows down, when would you estimate that it will stop growing altogether?
- What can you tell me about the growth of your bean from looking at this graph?

Another idea might be to interpret graphs from either textbooks or the internet relating to a contrasting locality being studied in geography. When teaching a Y3 class about Burkina Faso, the class studied a range of different graphs relating to annual rainfall, temperatures, life expectancies and such like. Linking this topic with the related numeracy objectives allows for a more cross-curricular approach and actually frees up time in the week for other teaching. This also introduces the children to the idea that learning about graphs is a valid and useful activity, rather than a skill learned in isolation.

Task

Consider the topics you have recently taught in science, geography and history. In which of these could you have taught graphical representations? You may find it useful to read Chapter 10 in conjunction with your thinking about graphical representation and interpreting data across the curriculum, in particular the section about the links with history.

Problem solving

Any of the NNS objectives relating to real life problems can easily be taught creatively. Long lists of word problems about money do not interest most children and do nothing to develop their own creativity either. Learning from the practical experiences provided in the Foundation Stage, teachers of even Y6 children can consider new ways of consolidating knowledge of money. Practical, *real* problems such as planning a Christmas party, or refreshments for sports day, can involve a wide range of skills from estimation, to money to measuring. Ratio also comes into the scenario, for example how many tubs of butter will be needed if two loaves use one tub and we are going to need 16 loaves? How much cheese? This is more likely to encourage children to think beyond the immediate question and create questions of their own.

One excellent example observed was a piece of work, which lasted all week in a mixed Y5/6 class. The theme was holidays and a lot of geographical work was also included. Each pair of children was given a budget in sterling and they had to put together a holiday package by looking at local tourist websites, airlines, car hire, etc. Most of the information they were accessing was in foreign currency so they had to convert the prices into sterling in order to keep track of how much they had 'spent'. Some of the more able children considered restaurant prices, fuel costs, and calculated distances from maps and even went onto sites for local attractions to cost daily activities. At the end of the week each pair discussed how they had allocated the money. Although they clearly could not then go on the holiday, they all felt that there had been a real purpose to their work and the amount of mathematics they had used was remarkable. A display was made of this work and it became a talking point amongst the whole school.

Task

Look at the learning objectives for money in Y3 and Y4. What activities could you provide instead of using worksheets? How would you ensure adequate differentiation?

Another obvious area of mathematics, which does not need to be completed by worksheets, is measures. Thankfully this is frequently done practically but there are still mathematics schemes which ask children to measure lines on the pages. Yes, this means that marking is easy as the answers all appear in the same order for every child, but even putting a tray of items on the desks for children to select is more interesting. Linking measuring to the party idea earlier in this chapter is another way of being a little more creative. Making cakes, sandwich fillings, biscuits and so forth are all wonderfully sensible ways to use measuring skills, as were growing the beans in the science example.

Differentiation

Another way of thinking about activities and avoiding the use of worksheets is to consider what kind of differentiation is needed to meet the diversity of needs within any class.

Differentiation can be achieved through:

Task

With worksheets the groups may be given different worksheets with different tasks to complete. In mathematics an obvious area is the size of numbers that different groups use to enable some children to be challenged by working with larger numbers in their calculations. If the children are using dice, for example, to decide upon the number they are taking away from a given number then the task shifts from being a reinforcement of existing calculations already written on a worksheet to exploring and investigating patterns in subtraction.

Through teaching

There are a number of different ways in which differentiation can be achieved through teaching. At a simple level this may be the questioning used within the lesson which challenges individuals appropriately. It may also be that some groups within the class are given a brief input to the task and asked to complete without further input but other groups may have more direct teaching time with more worked examples and support. Within the main activity phase of the lesson this could be that half the class are given a task to do whilst the rest of the class are directly taught the next steps or the time is used to reinforce previous concepts.

Interest

Unfortunately mathematics is not everyone's favourite subject but it is possible to create interest in the subject through use of individual or group interests and show the usefulness of mathematics. Looking at football results and how they are calculated may be an interest hook for a group of boys or one of the problem solving examples mentioned earlier in this chapter.

Outcome

Children can all be given the same task but different outcomes can be expected. This is not the same as output which is a direct measure of the amount of work completed. Differentiation by outcome focuses more on the learning rather than task completion.

Adult support

Adult support is more common in most classrooms and Early Years settings than ever before. This adult support comes in different guises; the adult could be a trainee teacher, a classroom teaching assistant, a learning mentor, a speech therapist or the class teacher. The key issue here is which adult support is the most appropriate for the task given to the class, group or individual that will enable the child(ren) to complete and extend the task. The adult is there not just to scaffold the learning for the specific task but to also provide a level of appropriate challenge whether the learners are playing in the Foundation stage or in a specific mathematics lesson in Y6.

Resource support

One way of looking at this is at the individual level and consider what additional resources might be needed to allow access to a task by all children. This might mean the instructions on a tape for a child who finds instructions hard to remember or it might be a multiplication table to support a learner who has difficulties remembering the facts but could, with the additional resource, complete the task that uses table facts as part of the process. The addition resources might offer a different level of challenge for an individual and/or group – at a simple level an additional question, another dice, another container; in other words, anything that will alter the original task to provide the challenge.

Technology

This has increased recently and there is a wide range of potential materials to support differentiation. See Table 4.1 on page 54.

Grouping

The most obvious grouping is by ability but mixed ability groupings can provide a different level of support and challenge for all children involved. By allowing some mixed ability groupings this gives access to potential higher order thinking skills to the lower ability children. It can allow children to achieve in areas that they would not usually expect to within ability groupings.

Recording

This area is explored in more detail in Chapter 7 where writing about mathematics is discussed. There is a tendency to assume that mathematics is always recorded mainly in number form. Sometimes, challenging the most able to record just by using words or just pictures can differentiate the level of challenge within the task. Restricting the ways to record can provide a very different challenge or considering the sense of audience as in literacy might be another way of thinking about recording expected. For younger learners, picking a favourite number sentence from their work or the sentence that gives the largest answer or the smallest might be the only recording expected. The latter example could be used in a review of the lesson to compare sentences chosen before they are displayed for future reference.

Role within group

Children can be assigned roles within a group activity which may mean the group would need to consider how it will record the evidence from their task. This method also gives children practise with specific roles which may challenge or support their existing strengths.

(Adapted from Briggs 2001)

Table 4.1 Examples of types of technology

Category	Examples
Drill and practice software on a computer	This enables either individuals to practise skills that they need support with or to extend the level of challenge for those who already have quick fact recall.
ILS: Integrated Learning Systems on a computer	Again, the focus is on the individual where practising skills can enable progress to be measured against previous achievements
Mathematics adventure and problem solving	Provides an interest to solve problems/tasks/activities and can be used with individuals/groups and/or class
Logo either on a computer including an IWB or a programmable toy	These can be used to provide a level of support and/or challenge to differentiate particularly shape and space activities.
Data handling software	These can be used to support activities like those described earlier in the chapter and lead children into active graphing.
Miscellaneous small software	These can provide extension activities and/or group activities that provide opportunities to focus on children's interests and/or to offer the opportunity for discussion during working on mathematical tasks.
Other devices, OHP, OHP calculator, IWB	These other devices offer a different image for children who may be visual learners. With IWB activities the fact that actions can be observed and completed by the learners supports kinaesthetic learners.
Websites	Website material can support children's investigations into currency exchanges around the world or to find problems to solve as simple examples.

Task

Consider how you differentiate activities for the class you are working with. Explore differentiating through an approach that you have not previously tried. If you start with the methods of differentiation does that also allow you to move away from using worksheets?

Resources

Ofsted (2003) discuss the 'ability of resources to raise the creative potential of a lesson' and this is an important issue for developing creative teaching and moving away from the use of worksheets. Collecting resources to enable worksheet ideas to become a more practically focused interactive lesson can be time-consuming and requires thought about the storage of the resources. The resources do not need to be expensive but could be a collection of fancy paper bags for presents or a collection of boxes to hold items for a game. Collections of dice for making number sentences, including blank ones, are a must as these are resources you can use time and time again. You don't have to photocopy these resources but can use them time and time again.

The following are just a few suggestions for a starting point of resources for a more creative approach to teaching:

- dice – for choosing numbers for calculations, games, chance
- collection of boxes – which can be either containers for items for an activity or can be filled with numbers of items for estimating, counting, weighing and measuring
- collections of bags – for sorting, collections, ordering
- dominoes – games (see Chapter 8), ordering fractions (if used for that, the line between the two halves is horizontal)
- small soft toys – for sorting, representing people for sharing
- items from a toy shop for pricing, with baskets and shopping lists (see role-play in Chapter 5 for more detail)
- collections of parcels in different shapes and sizes.

This chapter has tried to show the extent to which it is possible to creatively teach mathematics without the use of worksheets. It is not designed to give an exhaustive list of the ways this can be done but to offer a range of starting points to stimulate reflection upon current teaching practices and the potential to change. The key areas within the chapter are the starting points for activities, what makes a good activity and how do these link to differentiation and the need for match and challenge for all learners.

CHAPTER 5

Role-play

Role-play is an activity that most people immediately link to the Early Years. People think of small children in a role-play environment and usually some kind of shop for mathematics teaching and learning. This chapter will look at Early Years role-play for mathematics but it will also look at role-play for older children as well.

Why use role-play in teaching and learning mathematics?

- Role-play can motivate children to engage in activities.
- Role-play can motivate children to learn.
- The creative aspect of the role-play will make it seem more like play than like work.
- Role-play can allow children the opportunity to solve a problem or to resolve a conflict for their character and this can motivate a child. It is far more typical of the pressure that will be on them in real life.
- Role-playing environments are particularly useful in linking the using and applying of mathematics in different situations.
- Role-play can augment the traditional mathematics curricula for all age groups.
- The role-playing activities can enable children to look at the mathematics they are learning in a new light.
- Role-playing activities show the world as a complex place with complicated problems that can only rarely be solved by a simple answer that the children can previously have memorized.
- Through role-play children learn that skills they may learn separately are often used together in order to accomplish many real-world tasks.
- Sessions and lessons can use role-playing to emphasise the value of feelings and of creativity as well as of knowledge.

- Role-play offers the opportunity to practise 'real-world skills' in the safe situation in the classroom.
- Role-play activities can be used to develop skills important inside and outside of mathematics. Many of these are very difficult to teach using more traditional methods of instruction: self-awareness, problem solving, communication, initiative, teamwork.
- If a role-play environment includes research or problem solving, children are more likely to retain knowledge that they have constructed themselves than that simply handed to them in other classroom activities.

Burton (1990) suggested that there are key components of experience that she sees as central to learning mathematics. They are:

- accessibility
- engagement
- intellectual challenge
- satisfaction that comes from surmounting the challenge.

Good role-play should include all of these elements for the learners. You may find it helpful to keep these components in mind as you read the suggested examples of role-play in this chapter and your own work on establishing role-play as part of the teaching and learning of mathematics.

The following examples are role-play situations established to offer opportunities for children to learn across the curriculum but with the emphasis on mathematics.

Picnics

The class observed was a mixed group of 30 reception and Y1 children. As part of the ongoing topic, a picnic had been planned for that day, but the weather meant this was to be an indoor event. The children had discussed what a picnic was and their experiences of going on picnics, before the planning and preparation. There were a number of mathematically based activities from picnics about shape and space, fractions and number, particularly money.

Sandwiches

Each group of children were going to have the opportunity of making 'real' sandwiches to eat at lunch time. The fillings for the sandwiches included cress which had been grown in the class for this purpose. Another activity was to be looking at cutting sandwiches into different shapes and a different number of shapes that this would make. A piece of brown bread was represented by a square piece of brown paper for activities away from the real sandwich making which offered opportunities for mathematical modelling. Children were asked 'How would you make this into a triangle?' and 'Fold the paper and cut into triangles and make it back into a square again.'

Children were grouped to make sandwiches with paper. Children were asked to fold the paper to make a triangle. The adult asked the children if the children could make her a 4-triangle sandwich. The children moved around the groups to make real and paper sandwiches emphasising the shapes made in different ways, either squares or triangles.

Sausage rolls

Other groups were making real and imaginary sausages rolls. Questions were used to focus children's attention on the shape and amount of pastry to make sausage rolls. How much pastry is needed for the sausage roll? The adult and children discussed how sausage rolls are made. For a mathematical perspective there was use of imagery, shape, space and non-standard measures. Children made plasticine sausages and rolled out amounts of rectangular plasticine pastry to cover each of the sausages.

Carrying the picnic food

The children were asked 'How could you carry the food to the picnic?' and 'What sort of containers would you use for a sausage roll or a sandwich?' Children were able to be creative about their choice of containers from cuboids or cube boxes to one child who wanted a triangular prism for the triangle sandwiches.

Cakes

On the group making plasticine cakes, one child was making a long cylinder to make this cake. The child made connections between a story about living in a lighthouse yesterday and the spiral staircase in the lighthouse. The cake was going to be the same shape as the staircase. Other groups were making and decorating cakes which involved weighing and mixing ingredients.

The playing with a picnic in the classroom

The whole class was involved in getting the classroom ready for the picnic. The tables and chairs were moved to create space on the carpet area for the picnic. A table cloth was placed on the carpet and children went in small groups to wash their hands. The children then sat in a circle for the picnic. The teacher laid out the cloth and asked the children what the shape was. The table cloth was folded and again and again to form triangles. Each time the folding took place the children were asked about the shapes and sizes. Each child had a small table cloth that they could fold at the same time.

A number line was displayed from 1–8. Each item available at the picnic had been given a number. (The sandwich fillings were chosen by the children.)

1 cress sandwiches
2 cress and jam sandwiches
3 cheese sandwiches
4 cheese and cress sandwiches
5 just buttered bread
6 jam sandwiches
7 cakes
8 drinks

Shops in the classroom and in the outdoors

One of the most usual mathematical role-play environments that is created is a shop with a focus on money. However, if you have ever listened to small children in shop environments, bread for example can cost as much as a million pounds and you still get change! Any shop ideally needs real money to make the children feel that they are actually shopping.

Haberdashery (an interesting word to explore as a bonus of the role-play)
Resources needed: buttons on cards, wool, zips, fasteners, tape measures, ribbons, scissors, Velcro, pins and needles, crochet hooks, knitting needles, sequins, bias binding, beads, appliqué and motifs, cord, feather, elastic, fringing, poppers and studs.
   Mathematical activities possible: counting buttons on cards, beads and/or sequins, measuring any of the items to be sold by length, as well as cost, change and application of money.

Shoe shop
Resources needed: shoes, slippers, boots, shoe bags and boxes, trainers, shoe measures, shoe horns.
   Mathematical activities possible: shoe size UK or continental, what the relationship is between the measures, pairs, counting in twos, two times table, stocktaking, matching shoes and boxes.

Supermarket
Resources needed: tins of food, play food items, counter, till, money, swipe for cards, food trays, healthy biscuits and/or fruit to sell each day before breaks.
   Mathematical activities possible: quantity, money, each child has a purse or wallet with money to spend in the shop.

Travel agency
Resources needed: holiday catalogues, maps, tickets, telephone.

Mathematical activities possible: measures of distance travelled, time for journeys, changes of time across time zones, weight of luggage.

Garden shop (this can be inside, or outside it can become a garden centre)
Resources needed: plants, trowels, plastic flowers, seed packets, watering cans, seed trays, canes, sieve, bags of compost or substitute.

Mathematical activities possible: counting flowers, plants, seeds, money to pay for goods, quantities of compost to fill pots, language of full, half full and empty.

Builders yard (a great one for outside and getting boys involved in role-play)
Resources needed: builders trays, sand, gravel, spades, wheelbarrows, hard hats, buckets, wood, nails, play and/or real bricks, trowels, cones, small cars, clipboards, tape measures.

Mathematical activities possible: matching and counting equipment, measures, language of full, half full and empty, spadefuls to fill a bucket, stocktaking and ordering.

Flower shop
Resources needed: flowers, paper for bouquets, money, delivery van, bows, ribbons, cards.

Mathematical activities possible: counting, matching, estimating the amount of paper to make a bouquet of flowers.

Ice cream van (this can be inside or outside)
Resources needed: cones, tubs, scoops, sprinkles, flakes, sauces.

Mathematical activities possible: counting, matching, money including change.

Post office (although not strictly a shop, often within a shop not on their own)
Resources needed: letters, stamps, scales, measures for envelope sizes, parcels, uniforms.

Mathematical activities possible: comparisons of size and weight, cost of stamps, distance travelled between where something is posted and where it is sent to.

There are clearly some health and safety issues that need to be considered before setting up the role-play which can either be indoors or outdoors. Some times a role-play may have two parts, for example the builders yard outside, the site office or show house inside, so the role-plays can be connected between the environments and engage different groups of children in a wide range of activities. In each of the role-plays suggested as a starting point here there will be opportunities for learning across the curriculum and not just mathematical skills and knowledge, even though that is the emphasis in this book.

Task

Task

If you are not an Early Years teacher or you work with older children it is worth visiting an Early Years class or unit to see how a good role-play area needs to be resourced to make it an effective environment for learning. If you can visit make a note of the resources that are available for the children.

Resources

Resources for role-play are an essential part of the planning. If you have storage facilities available then collecting resources when you see them can be helpful with later planning. The following is a list of initial resources that are worth collecting to support the learning and teaching of mathematics in role-play:

- baskets of different sizes, colours and shapes
- boxes of different shapes and sizes, with and without lids
- bricks of all kinds, shapes and sizes (for building large or scale models as part of role-play)
- games from other countries and throughout history, including Senet
- mathematical equipment from other countries and through history including Soroban, slide rules, slates
- measuring equipment old and new, some of these may not be used in more traditional mathematical sessions/lessons
- money, preferably real, with purses and wallets
- telephones of different types.

Task

Look around the environment you are working in and the resources that are available. Do you know what is there? What would you want to collect to enrich these resources?

Role-playing other situations that involve mathematics

Tenpin bowling

Either in a space indoors or outdoors children can take on the roles associated with activities like tenpin bowling. Children can be in charge of setting up the pins, organising the teams and keeping the scores. Games like this can be played with the

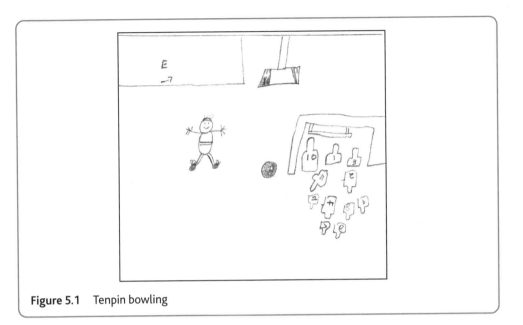

Figure 5.1 Tenpin bowling

normal rules and scoring or they can be changed to offer the opportunity to use and apply calculation skills and knowledge learnt in the classroom. Other children could be involved in extending the role-play to include the sale of drinks and snacks.

Role-play with links across the curriculum

Becoming an Egyptian

Role-play for older children in KS2 can take over the whole class and the timetable for a given amount of time. This means that the role-play is not always available as it might be in the early years. Although this may not be ideal it gives role-play a different and potentially more 'grown up' emphasis for the older children. Space can be a difficulty for classes of older children and so a specific time for role-play can be a useful way to integrate this approach into the learning and teaching. As part of an integral role-play, whilst studying the Egyptians children can examine the measuring units used by the ancient Egyptians and decide which ones to apply in order to measure various objects. They can compare ancient measuring units with modern measuring units and recognise the imperfections of the ancient units. The children can look at the way numbers were written in Ancient Egypt and may complete simple calculations using this system. Children examine the measuring units used by the ancient Egyptians and decide which ones to apply in order to measure various objects. They can compare ancient measuring units, based on the width of a finger, a span of the hand and the length of your forearm, with modern measuring units and potentially recognise the imperfections of the ancient units. During this role-play they can measure various objects on display, as well as themselves. Resources can be borrowed from local library and history services to give children replica arte-facts to work with.

Children can also look at the way numbers were written in Ancient Egypt and complete simple and more complicated calculations using this system. This gives opportunities for connections between addition and subtraction and multiplication and division to be made. Other activities could cover topics such as mirror images, reflection, co-ordinates, symmetry and repeated patterning. Children can develop strategy and team-building skills while playing the ancient board game called Senet (see Figure 5.2).

How to play Senet
→ direction of initial play, the counters then zigzag towards the finish
→ direction to the finish

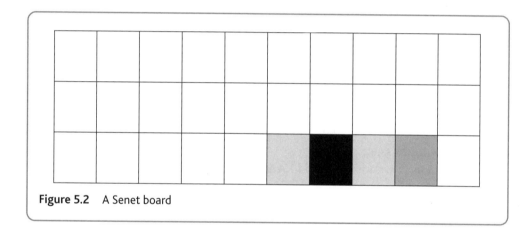

Figure 5.2   A Senet board

1 Throw the sticks to see how many squares to move your piece forward.

2 If you throw a one, four, or six, you get an extra turn. The number of sticks thrown is based on a darker and lighter side to show which side lands uppermost. You count the darker sides showing to indicate the number of spaces you can move.

3 You can't land on one of your own pieces.

4 If you land on the other player's piece, you switch places with them. However, you can't switch with them if they have two or more pieces in a row.

5 If the other player has three or more pieces in a row, you can't pass them.

6 Some squares are 'safe' squares and some are 'danger' squares. You will learn what they are as you play. These are the ones with hieroglyphics on them; in the

diagram of the board the bad is the dark shaded square and the lighter shaded squares have safe symbols on.

7   The first player to get all of their pieces off the board wins the game. This has to be by the exact number of spaces to move.

(Rules taken from www.ancientegypt.co.uk/life/activity/main.html which is part of the British Museum site where an interactive version of the game can be played.)

A replica of a Senet board found in Tutankhamen's tomb could be used and the children can throw sticks as well as a die to encourage them to explore probability. Children could also build pyramids using multi-link blocks and work out everyday mathematical problems of the ancient embalmer and their need to use measures. Children can be encouraged to explore number patterns, make predictions and develop mathematical strategies to overcome difficulties as they work on the activities.

Another activity they might try is to solve the puzzle from Ancient Egypt and recorded by the scribe Ahmes on the Rhind papyrus 1850 BC. A wealthy Egyptian farmer owned seven wheat stores. Each of the wheat stores housed seven cats. Each of the cats caught seven rats. Each rat would have eaten seven sheaves of wheat. Each sheave of wheat produced seven measures of flour. How many measures of flour did the farmer's cats save?

Since calculators weren't around in Ancient Egypt, this is a pencil and paper calculation and then a calculator for checking. The answer to this puzzle comes from doing the following calculations. There are a total of 49 cats (7×7) in the seven barns. The 49 cats caught 343 mice (49×7 or $7 \times 7 \times 7$). The 343 mice would have eaten 2,401 sheaves of wheat (343×7 or $7 \times 7 \times 7 \times 7$). The 2,401 sheaves of wheat produced 16,807 measures of flour ($2,401 \times 7$ or $7 \times 7 \times 7 \times 7 \times 7$), which is the answer to this ancient puzzle.

Becoming an Ancient Greek

Greeks are world-renowned as some of the greater mathematicians. In this role-play the children take on the role of Greek mathematicians to solve challenges such as follows:

- As well as being good mathematicians Greeks were good builders. Solve this building challenge – using polydron or similar pieces to build 3-D shapes, a closed shape using 2 triangles and 3 squares, a closed shape using 6 squares and 2 hexagons, a closed shape using 4 triangles and 5 squares.

- Solve Athena's puzzle – Athena wants to go back to Mount Olympus. To do so she must arrange 12 pentomino pieces into a rectangle.
- Solve Zeus' Challenge – This is a two-person game. Players take turns placing a pentomino piece in a rectangle board. The pieces could not overlap or extend outside the rectangle. The *last* person to place a piece is the winner.

A trip around the world

In this activity the children all have a passport in which they collect stamps from each country they will visit in the setting, class or school. In this role-play the children are explorers and on their travels they have to solve or have a go at activities selected appropriately for their age group that come from a selection of different countries. The activities are set out around the space allocated and adults with each of the activities. Each child travels around the activities and gains a stamp when completed.

- China – may be a dice activity or tangrams
- Egypt – play a game of Senet
- England – play Nine Men's Morris
- Japan – Sudoku puzzle
- Africa – play Wari
- Germany – solve Dürer's magic square

An additional activity would be to work out the distance travelled depending upon the route around the countries and the time zone differences between GMT and the country visited. The number of countries and the type of activities depend upon the age of the children, the available space and number of adults. This could be an activity for the whole school where each class is a particular country and all children visit to try activities, puzzles and games as they travel the world.

Although focusing principally on the humanities, another source of starting points for role-plays with any age group would be the 'Mantle of the Expert', more details are available from www.mantleoftheexpert.com

Task

Consider your own starting point for a role-play with the children you work with. Consider the resources that are needed and the mathematical activities that will form the basis of the opportunities you will be planning. How might you involve the children in planning the time you will allocate to the activity?

Television and films as a stimulus for role-play

Treasure Hunt

In this game of strategy and roles each of the children in the class take the role of the treasure hunters. Here there could be links with Lara Croft in *Tomb Raider*, US films like *Raiders of the Lost Ark* and *National Treasure* or the television series *Relic Hunter* about a professor of archaeology who is also a treasure hunter. Each team must collect a set amount of treasure to win the game. This could be set up to emphasise exchange from units into tens and hundreds. The children could either find the treasure through solving clues in teams, or the treasure could be the prize for problems solved correctly. This could include making shapes from nets or a range of shapes to make others.

> ### Task
> Plan a treasure hunt type of role-play for teams in the class. Decide how the children will win the treasure and how they will exchange the amounts at a bank, for example.

Use of technology to create the environment for role-play

Professor Steven Heppell's work on the use of technology to develop teaching and learning offers us an example of how role-play may develop further beyond the traditional interpretation. The 'Be Very Afraid' website (www.heppell.net/bva) showcases innovative practices in the use of technologies to support learning. Selections of these projects are showcased at BAFTA each year. The advisors with teachers at Matching Green school set up a project to rescue a computer called OM2 within a space station which has collapsed and the children's task was to bring the computer back on line, involving answering questions to challenges received through a mobile phone call. The challenges in this case link to literacy and numeracy and creating a very different kind of role-play which could be adapted if the technology is available to create a situation for offering a stimulating environment for children's learning. The children working on this role-play were Y4.

> ### Task
> Plan a series of questions to free a computer and teach it different aspects of mathematics so it learns. The children could take on the role of computer engineers who are teaching the computer. It may be a good idea to have more than one computer that needs to be taught different aspects of mathematics to meet the diversity of children's needs. Alternatively the children may work in mixed ability groups to solve the tasks so drawing on skills within the team. How might you include the use of mobile technology in any role play?

Role-play involving teams including taking on a specific role

Being a bee

In this role-play each team of children, now bees, have a task to make a hive with newspaper, scissors and sticky tape as the only resources. This role-play could be part of work on looking at insects but could be a separate role-play to emphasise shape and space. Depending upon the class, you might give each team some information to help their role-play as worker bees. They would need a time limit for their building time. The mathematical focus here is shape and space.

Family of elephants

In this role-play the teams of children are elephants and must find out about the relative size of elephants and how big their footprints would be. Which doors would they be able to get through in the school? How many elephants could fit into the class? This role-play could involve researching information about elephants, what they eat, how much they need to eat each day, what that would look like, how they could model this, how big they are and presenting the information from their research in the role of a family of elephants. The mathematical focus here is measures, linear, capacity, modelling and comparison.

Editorial team

In this role-play the class as a whole work as an editorial team to publish a mathematical dictionary or a book about an aspect of mathematics that they are working on. Different roles could be allocated to smaller teams within the class, such as illustrations, definitions and layout. This could involve the use of computers to type the written information and scan in drawings before publishing.

> *Task*
>
> Plan a team style role-play either from one of the starting points suggested or from one of your own.

This chapter has explored the ideas of role-play and suggested that although traditionally seen as the preserve of the Early Years it is a creative approach to working across the age range. Role-play can, to quote Burton (1990), be accessible, ensure engagement and offer intellectual challenge and satisfaction that comes from surmounting the challenge.

Stories and other literature sources

This chapter looks at the using of stories and other literature sources as a starting point for creative teaching and learning of mathematics. The Every Child Matters (ECM) agenda is about removing barriers to children's learning and finding alternative approaches to teaching and learning that enables all children to achieve. Stories can be one way into removing those barriers for some children. In addition, with the Primary National Strategy focus on cross-curricular working, the combination of literature and mathematics is a timely consideration.

Literature offers an opportunity to link often abstract mathematical ideas with other events in children's everyday lives. All early mathematical ideas, though, take shape through children's attempts to communicate as they explore their environments and as a result, mathematical ideas have found their way into literature. People have an inherent sense of number (Dehaene 1997) and so mathematical ideas are expressed in stories, essays, poems, books, and other forms of literature. One way of facilitating the connection between school mathematics and everyday life then is to use the mathematics embedded in the children's literature.

There are a number of commercial mathematics schemes that offer specific literature texts to support the teaching of key concepts as part of the range of resources. One such scheme is published by Kingscourt, which offers storybooks around topics like subtraction and division. It also includes books that provide general information and non-fiction materials on topics like money. These are intended to be support for the whole class introduction to topic areas. These also have ideas for activities linked to the mathematical topic.

What are the benefits of using children's literature to teach mathematics?

Linking mathematics teaching with children's literature has moved in and out of popularity for a variety of reasons. Some of the negative reasons have been linked to the introduction of the numeracy strategy and the feeling that the three-part lesson structure did not allow for the use of stories. Some positive reasons suggest that the literature connection motivates children, particularly the older Primary ages, to engage with mathematics (Usnick and McCarthy 1998). Welchman-Tischler (1992) suggests it promotes interest and helps children connect mathematical ideas to their personal experiences. Others suggest that the use of literature accommodates children with different learning styles, promotes critical thinking or provides a context for using mathematics to solve problems, which can be given different cultural contexts by the specific choice of literature. Most of the benefits are related through specific accounts from teachers and other adults working with children; there is relatively little formal evidence presented for the benefits of use of literature within mathematics. Hong (1996) did find that nursery-aged children who were exposed to story-related mathematics exhibited a greater preference and aptitude for mathematics activities than did those of a comparison group.

What makes a good book to use for mathematics?

The following are some suggestions for deciding whether a book is suitable to use for the learning and teaching of mathematics. Criteria for evaluating children's books with mathematical dimensions have been suggested by Austin (1998). The first issue she discusses is that any book chosen for use should provide a quality, pleasurable and authentic literary experience as well as the opportunity to use mathematics for authentic purposes. The context of the book is very important, as without a context the mathematics can appear meaningless. Even if this is counting animals, there is a reason for the action needed, for example the farmer is checking how many sheep they have and if they have lost any. This kind of action allows children to see that there is a purpose behind the task; in this case counting has a purpose – the farmer can tell if they have lost any sheep. A child who has had this kind of experience is less likely, when asked about why they count, to answer, 'My teacher tells me to.' So a checklist for a good book to use with mathematics would have to include context and the book to be a quality literary experience, but what else?

- context of the mathematics is meaningful
- quality of literary experience is good
- the children can engage with the characters in the book where appropriate
- the children can engage with the mathematics
- the activities from the book can be accessible to all
- the activities from the book can offer an appropriate level of challenge
- the activities from the book can be fun
- the activities from the book can be returned to and expanded
- the activities from the book are not tokenistic.

All classrooms have children's books which can be used as a stimulus to support not just the creative teaching approaches but also children's creative thinking in mathematics. This chapter offers some suggestions for the use of children's books with different age groups. These are not special resources but ordinary books that are available in most schools. If the specific book is not available then the principles used to develop the work here can be applied to other similar texts.

Jim and the Beanstalk

This example comes from a trainee teacher working with her class teacher in a reception class. The school is multicultural and is developing the use of the outdoors in the Early Years. This was a series of lessons with a story as an initial focus for the children's activities. Previously the children had worked on *Goldilocks and the Three Bears*. During this week the children had been read the story of *Jim and the Beanstalk* and then activities were linked to areas of learning for the children. Figure 6.1 shows the lesson plan for this activity (see pp. 72–3).

The activities with the whole class are focused on the use of language: small, smallest, large and largest. Resources were made for the children to assist their visualisation of the differences between the items. The children were involved from the start with painting a giant for the wall.

The Queen's Knickers

Humour can be a great way to engage children in their learning especially if the subject matter is seen by them as slightly risqué or rude. In this case the focus is knickers which always make young children laugh. The story is about the loss of a chest full of the Queen's knickers. The Queen has different knickers for different occasions. Instead of taking specific aspects from the story it can be used as a starting point for a combinatorix problem. The children in Y1 or Y2 are given specific instructions about the limit of colours or designs that might be provided for the Queen and the idea is to exhaust the possible combinations without repeats.

The same kind of problems can be linked to other books like *Stanley Bagshaw and the Short-sighted Goalkeeper* for combinations of football strips or *The Snowman* for combinations of snowmen with hats, scarf and nose.

In some texts, these are seen as problem solving examples yet they have a specific outcome, which is very different from solving problems that may have numerous potential outcomes. In many ways, these combinatorix problems are very close in relation to the creative aspects of mathematics. The focus here is on creative and stimulating teaching of a closed area of mathematics. A booklist of suitable stories, with mathematics areas covered, can be found on pages 78–81.

Some scheme's materials have large text versions of books. The following are some examples all published by Kingscourt:

- *Ten Tiny Ants* by Rosemary Reville Irons and focusing on reciting numbers in order, forwards and backwards
- *Buzzing Bees* by Rosemary Reville Irons and focusing on understanding the link between addition and subtraction
- *The Dancing Dragons* by Calvin Irons and focusing on reciting numbers in order
- *Muffins at the Fair* by Calvin Irons and focusing on understanding the relationship between multiplication and division
- *The Puppet Party* by Rosemary Reville Irons and focusing on reciting number names in order
- *The Squirrel's Store* by Rosemary Reville Irons and focusing on counting, reciting numbers 1–5
- *Wayne's New Shape* by Calvin Irons and focusing on 3-D shapes.

These books are designed to be a stimulus for introducing a new topic and offering opportunities to practise skills. Each of these books has lesson plans and worksheets to assist teachers in the final pages of the book.

Reading scheme materials

Other readily available stories that can be a resource are reading scheme books. These have the advantage of being familiar to children in relation to the vocabulary used, the characters and the story lines. The children can also read these themselves. Although not used in all schools, The Oxford Reading Tree scheme has provide a familiar format for stories involving Kipper, Biff, Chip and Floppy the dog. They are moved from situation to situation by the means of a glowing magic key. This format could be a useful one for planning mathematics lessons for a class familiar with the stories. The magic key could take the whole class to a different time to find out about a mathematician or specific event like the introduction of Babbage's counting machine. The magic key might take the children to a land of particular shapes, Hexagon Haven for example, where everything is made of hexagons. This becomes the stimulus for children to create the world within the classroom and consider how to draw hexagons of different sizes and what ordinary things would look like in this hexagon world. Alternatively, the magic key could become a series of keys to be won by solving calculations and other problems to enable a team or an individual to open a box. Yet another alternative could be to use the keys for a box scenario and plan a logic problem with keys to open a box. This is turn links to the logic problem set for *Alice in Wonderland* and the potions and cakes problem or the potions riddle in *Harry Potter and the Philosopher's Stone* solved by Hermione.

Group / Class Reception	Number of children 27	Day/Date	Time 9.15-9.40

Focus Activity: Mathematical development- comparative language

Area(s) of learning
CLL
MD

QCA early learning goals for focus areas of learning
CLL- Language for communication
MD- Shape, space and measures

Children's previous experience:
Children are beginning to use comparative language. They have recently spent a week doing a mini project on Goldilocks and the Three Bears and are regularly exposed to play situations aimed at developing comparative language.

Notes from previous lesson(s) from assessment including errors and misconceptions that need to addressed in this lesson:
Children need further activities in this area to reinforce and extend their learning.

QTS standards for observation

Stepping Stones/ELGs refs	Learning objectives
CLL- Sustain attentive listening, responding to what they have heard by relevant comments, questions or actions. -Respond to simple instructions -Describe main story settings, events and principal characters MD- Use language such as 'greater', 'smaller', 'heavier', 'lighter' to compare quantities - Use size language such as 'big' and 'little'. - Order 2/3 items by length/height.	-To use comparative language to describe giant's glasses, teeth, wig - To order glasses, teeth, hair/children in terms of size (smallest to largest) - To suggest which items will fit giant

Assessment: learning outcomes to be monitored
Targeted questioning and observation (notes will be made at the end of the session) will help to inform future planning. TA to observe and make notes on a focused group during session.

Figure 6.1 Lesson plan for *Jim and the Beanstalk*

Information on the organisation of group/s undertaking the activity
Whole class session. Harj/Jaz to support Dilprit and Ajay on carpet (translating when necessary). Julie to sit near/support Jake and Amy (encourage participation, model vocabulary, ensure children maintaining attention). Mrs T to support Felicia, Bruna, Debora (ensure they are maintaining attention, translate).

Key vocabulary and questions
Giant, story, next, measure, tape measure, size, glasses, false teeth, wig, big, small, bigger, smaller, taller, shorter, order, smallest, biggest.
Who can remember what our story was about? How did Jim help the giant? What happened first? What did Jim use to measure the giant' eyes etc? What happened next? Which is the biggest/smallest pair of glasses/teeth/wig? Can you help me to put them into size order, from smallest to biggest? Which pair of glasses etc do you think will fit our giant? Who thinks they are bigger than our giant?

Structure of the activity	Teaching Points
Introduction	Recap on story. Chn to say what story was about. Teacher to go through book, asking children what happens next in the story- children to state how Jim helped the giant.
Main activity	Produce giant, pin him up on wall. Chn to suggest what giant is missing. Show glasses. 2 children to come to front to hold largest and smallest pair of glasses. Children to state which is smallest /biggest. Teacher to hold middle-sized pair- chn to put them into size order (smallest to largest). Repeat with other items. Ask chn which pair of glasses etc they think will fit the giant. Teacher to put items against giant to see if correct, put items into hoop. Seat children in circle, put giant in middle- chn to put glasses etc on to giant.
Finishing off / follow up	Put giant back onto wall. Ask who thinks they are bigger than giant. Measure 3 children against giant, put chn into size order (smallest to biggest). Praise efforts, inform children of groups for free flow session.

Lead practitioner role:
Monitor behaviour, ensure children know what is expected of them in terms of activity and behaviour, model vocabulary, target questioning, provide support as necessary, provide praise and verbal feedback.

Additional resources
Story- 'Jim and the Beanstalk', giant (made by children), glasses, teeth, wigs.

Figure 6.1 Continued

Task

Review the resources available in your setting/school. Does this include any large books to introduce topics to the class? Have you ever used these? Talk to colleagues to find out what their experiences are. If appropriate try one of these texts with your class. Think about what difference this made to your teaching and the engagement of the children with the activities.

Different ways to use children's books in teaching and learning mathematics

There are many children's books which are explicitly about mathematics, such as books about counting or shapes; other books have mathematics embedded within a larger context as has already been described. These books are generally not perceived as 'maths books' but mathematics appears as one element within stories and this can include problems, personal experiences and/or cultural events. Welchman-Tischler (1992) classified the ways to use these books as follows:

- To provide a context for an activity with mathematical content.
- To provide a context for a model with mathematical content.
- To introduce equipment/apparatus that will be used in varied ways (not necessarily as in the story).
- To inspire a creative mathematics experience for children.
- To pose an interesting problem.
- To prepare for a mathematics concept or skill.
- To develop or explain a mathematics concept or skill.
- To review a mathematics concept or skill.
- To allow children to pose their own problems from the story.
- To allow children to model in different ways their understanding of mathematical concepts.

(Adapted from Welchman-Tischler 1992)

Although books can be used in a number of different ways, the idea behind introducing them is to add interest and a stimulus to the learning and teaching of mathematics.

Books from other countries

Increasingly children come to Early Years settings and schools speaking a wide range of first languages other than English. One way of widening the experience of all children is to use resources from other countries. Table 6.1 gives a few ideas from a small range of materials.

Table 6.1 Books from other countries

Book	Context for exploration through mathematics
Viza, M and Rovira, F. (1987) *En Train*. Bordas.	This is a simple book in French, focusing on a train journey for a family, including on a sleeper. Distance, time and cost of tickets are potential areas to investigate through reading this book.
Αγκυρα (2003) Ο λύκος και τα εφτά κατοικάκια. Harmi Press	This is a story about a wolf and a family of goats who outsmart the wolf. A similar story to *The Three Little Pigs* without different houses.
Grace, P. (1993) *Te Toneke or The Trolley*. Puffin Books.	This story from New Zealand, available in Maori and English, is about making a go-cart and could be the source of linking science and mathematics through making and testing wheeled vehicles and measuring the distance travelled and timing their journeys.
Olonde, S. (1988) *Gitonga na Stono*. Sasa Sema Publications.	This story in cartoon form is from Kenya and is Kiswahilli, which involves four central characters and their journeys around Kenya, Ethiopia and Dubai. This is not for young children as the characters carry guns, big sticks and machetes!
Lampthorne, V., Mayor, J., Quilley, J., Lewis, B., Cameron, L. (1980, 1982) *Two Collections of Stories from Overseas, Two Tales from Tanzania and Tales from Kenya and Zambia*. Oxfam Group.	These books, as part of Oxfam resources for teachers, have tales from different countries in Africa. They offer suggestions about cross-curricular links with each story. The mathematical activities include calculations, data handling, capacity in relation to water needed to be collected, and time.

Task

What materials do you have available in different languages and from other countries? What mathematics might be linked with the materials? What other knowledge might children learn? For example, having to carry all the water you need several miles for everyday things like cooking, washing and drinking gives you a whole new perspective on being able to go to the tap in your house. This could lead to exploring the relationship between the volume of water and its weight. What kinds of containers would be best for carrying water without spilling it and making it easier to carry some distance?

Use of other sources of stories and scenarios to use as a stimulus for mathematics learning and teaching

Other sources of stories that can stimulate children to count, sort or to solve problems is the use of videos or DVDs. These can be used to provide the element of story in the same way as books can. Children's television programmes available on video/DVD can be a good source of potential stories. Table 6.2 offers a few examples of programme episodes and how they could be used as a starting point for mathematics.

Table 6.2   Children's television programmes

Series	Mathematical activities from the programme
Clangers – episode 'Goods' by Oliver Postgate made by Smallfilms. The episode involves a machine that makes many different types of goods.	sorting by size, colour, type of good produced
From the Old Bear stories by Jane Hissey – programme Ruff and the Big Wheel	comparisons of wheel sizes, circumference, radius, diameter
Postman Pat	parcels, weight, cost of postage, letters size, cost of postage
Pocoyo – 7 minute animations	one programme involved a chase through doors and mirrors, a potentially good introduction to reflections and rotations investigation
Bob the Builder by Keith Chapman	'Lofty and the Giant Carrot' for comparison and modelling. 'Bob's Big Plan' for drawing plans to scale.
The Simpsons	'Team Homer' episode about Homer putting together a bowling team, scoring, investigating teams, highest scores and averages.

Task

Choose a children's television episode or similar to plan a series of activities to engage children in a specific idea from the list of potential suggestions or from another programme that you have on video/DVD.

Films with stories to fire the imagination and offer starting points for mathematics

300

A recent film *300* has received a lot of attention and although the rating of the film places it outside the age ranges of Primary children the images and the interest this creates can be used especially to interest boys. *300* is based loosely according to historians on the Battle of Thermopylae of 480 BC where an alliance of Greek city-states fought the invading Persian Empire at the pass of Thermopylae in central Greece. The Greek forces and their allies were vastly outnumbered. The Greeks held back the Persians for three days with a small force led by King Leonidas of Sparta who blocked the only road through which the massive army of Xerxes could pass. After three days of battle, a local resident named Ephialtes betrayed the Greeks by revealing a mountain path that led behind the Greek lines. King Leonidas dismissed the rest of the army and stayed behind with 300 Spartans and 700 Thespian volunteers to hold the pass. The Persians finally succeeded in taking the pass but sustained much heavier losses than the Greeks sustained. Whilst the battle raged, Athens prepared for a naval battle that would come to determine the outcome of the war. Subsequent battles sent Xerxes and his forces home defeated on sea and land. The mathematical ratio of Spartan forces to Xerxes could be calculated through historical research. Distances could be measured for forces to march in a day.

Charlotte's Web

Another recently remade film is an adaptation of E.B. White's novel *Charlotte's Web*. Mathematical activities from this could include weighing pigs, making moneyboxes for pocket money like Fern. Finding out about the length and sizes of spiders from around the world would involve children in researching and presenting their data to show differences in length and size. Teams of children could be asked to research different animals in the story and present facts about them. If looking again at spiders, where the largest spiders are found and where the smallest are found would be questions that children could research. They could also begin to consider why the largest spiders might come from particular places. The shape of spiders' webs could also be researched and the length of thread that might be needed to make a web for a spider. Travelling spiders could be attached to balloons and let go like the baby spiders at the end of the book and, if return labels are attached to the balloons and spiders, children can plot how far the balloon spiders have travelled.

Night at the Museum

This comedy film may not immediately appear to offer stimulus for mathematical activities and creative experiences but hidden in the story are many opportunities for mathematics. Within the film there are a number of key historical events pictured which could be researched and a time line produced showing the relative dates. The large dinosaur Rex could be explored in relation to its size including the scale of its footprints and speed of movement. The scale of the dioramas of events in the museum could be a starting point for scaling of models for another event for display in the classroom. Writing mathematical rules for the night guard to follow could also be a starting point for investigating order. Children could find out where the American Museum of Natural History is, how they would get there, how much it would cost to get there, what the entry cost is, how old the building the museum is housed in is, for example.

This chapter is designed to 'whet the appetite' for the use of books and other sources of literature within mathematics sessions/lessons. The idea is to start the process of thinking about resources for mathematics learning and teaching outside the strategy and scheme materials and to focus on what interests children. This is a move back towards child-centred learning that has not disappeared from Early Years but has been largely ignored in the Primary years as a direct result of the separation of mathematics and the 'numeracy hour'. Although this has been good for mathematics and established an emphasis on mental and oral methods and conceptual understanding rather than procedural understanding, the experience for teachers and children has become rather 'samey' for each lesson. This does not mean, as expressed earlier in this book, that every lesson has to be all-singing all-dancing as that is unrealistic. This chapter will hopefully bring back some of the expertise and creativity in teaching mathematics and allow those with specific strength in their knowledge of books and other text resources to see the connections with mathematics and use those to enliven their teaching and the children's learning.

Table 6.3 Maths from stories: a mathematical booklist

Book	Mathematics areas covered
Bradman, T. (1991) *Goldilocks and the Three Bears*. Methuen.	counting (1–3), size comparison matching
Bang, M. (1987) *Ten, Nine, Eight*. Green Willow Books.	counting (1–10)
Lively, P. and Ormerod, J. (1999) *One, Two, Three Jump!* Puffin Books.	counting
Dale, P. (1996) *Ten in the Bed*. Walker.	counting (1–10)
Brown, M. (1991) *Witches Four*. Grosset & Dunlap.	counting (4), number story
Bradman, T. (1985) *The Bad Babies' Counting Book*. Piccadilly Press.	counting
Yeoman, J. and Blake, Q. (1971) *Sixes and Sevens*. MacMillan.	counting

Table 6.3 Continued

Book	Mathematics areas covered
Kusagak, M.A. (1999) *My Arctic 1 2 3*. Sagebrush.	counting
Carle, E. (1990) *1,2,3, to the Zoo*. Puffin Books.	counting
Crowther, R. (1986) *The Most Amazing Hide-and-Seek Numbers Book*. Viking Children's Books.	counting 1–100
Wylie, J. and D. (1987) *A Fishy Counting Story*. Children's Press.	counting (more and less than)
Beck, I. (1999) *Five Little Ducks*. Orchard Books.	concept of 'less one'
Burningham, J. (1983) *The Shopping Basket*. Picture Lions.	counting and subtracting
Blake, Q. (1999) *Mister Magnolia*. Red Fox.	pairs (odd/even)
Carle, E. (2002) *The Very Hungry Caterpillar*. Puffin Books.	counting, days, ordering
Kerr, J. (1991) *The Tiger who Came to Tea*. Picture Lions.	beginning to understand and use ordinal numbers
Burgess, M. (1994) *One Little Teddy Bear*. Picture Lions.	adding and subtracting from one number
Hutchins, P. (1989) *The Doorbell Rang*. Harper Trophy.	number story (factors of 12)
Inkpen, M. (1993) *Kipper's Toy Box*. Hodder Children's Books.	counting (within 15)
Browne, E. (1995) *Handa's Surprise*. Walker Books.	ordinal numbers, subtraction
Inkpen, M. (1993) *Billy's Beetle*. Hodder Children's Books.	beginning to understand vocabulary of addition and subtraction
Briggs, R. (1970) *Jim and the Beanstalk*. Hamish Hamilton/Puffin Books.	size, need to measure, scale for older children
Haswell, P. (1992) *Pog Climbs Mount Everest*. Walker Books.	fractions (Pog carries a ladder half way up)
Lipniacka, E. (1996) *To Bed . . . or Else!* Crocodile Books.	fractions, expand the time, two, two and a half
Hutchins, P. (1988) *One-Eyed Jake*. Puffin Books.	heavier, lighter, balance
West, C. (2001) *'Pardon?' Said the Giraffe*. Walker Books.	comparative sizes
Riddell, C. (1990) *The Trouble with Elephants*. Walker Books.	size, weight
Allen, P. *Who Sank the Boat?* (1988) Puffin Books.	comparing size and weight of different animals *(Continued)*

Table 6.3 Continued

Book	Mathematics areas covered
Ambrus, V.G. (1991) *What's the Time, Dracula?* Oxford University Press.	Dracula worries about a dentist's appointment at 3 o'clock
Murphy, J. (2006) *Five Minutes' Peace.* Walker Books.	passage of time
Hawkins, C. (1986) *What's the Time, Mr Wolf?* Picture Lions.	time (clock)
Hutchins, P. (1981) *Happy Birthday, Sam.* Puffin Books.	size and passage of time
Hawkins. C (1987) *Mr Wolf's Week.* Picture Lions.	days of the week
McLean, G. (2002) *Time to Get Up.* Tamarind.	days of week, time
Bacon, R. (2001) *Jessie's Flower.* Shortland Publications.	time, day and night, sequencing
Townson, H. and Ross, T. (1986) *Terrible Tuesday.* William Morrow.	days of the week
Hughes, S. (1997) *Alfie's Feet.* Red Fox.	left/right, right/wrong
Sutton, E. and Dodd, L. (1978) *My Cat Likes to Hide in Boxes.* Puffin Books.	3-D shapes
Waddell, M. (1996) *When the Teddy Bears Came.* Walker Books.	vocabulary describing position, size, data handling
Rosen, M. (1993) *We're Going on a Bear Hunt.* Walker Books.	position, direction and movement
Wylie, J. and D. (1989) *A Fishy Size Story.* Franklin Watts.	language for large
Berenstain, S. and J. (1982) *Inside, Outside, Upside Down.* Picture Lions.	positional language
Hutchins, P. (2001) *Rosie's Walk.* Red Fox.	positional language
Allen, P. (1994) *Mr Archimedes' Bath.* Puffin Books.	capacity
Ahlberg, J. (1984) *The Baby's Catalogue.* Puffin Books.	sorting and grouping
Rylands, L. (1988) *Some of Us.* Dinosaur Publications.	sorting
Hayes, S. and Ormerod, J. (1989) *Eat Up, Gemma.* Walker Books.	sorting, data handling
Waddell, M. (1995) *Farmer Duck.* Walker Books.	data handling
Ahlberg, A. (1981) *Master Money the Millionaire.* Puffin Books.	money
Hutchins, P. (1978) *Don't Forget the Bacon.* Puffin Books.	ordering, counting

Table 6.3 Continued

Book	Mathematics areas covered
Wilson, B. (2004) *Stanley Bagshaw and the Fourteen Foot Wheel*. Barn Owl Books.	various comparisons and measures
Wilson, B. (2005) *Stanley Bagshaw and the Twenty Two Ton Whale*. Barn Owl Books.	various comparisons and measures
Briggs, R. (2004) *The Snowman*. Puffin Books.	sequencing and combinatorix
Allen, N. (1993) *The Queen's Knickers*. Red Fox.	combinatorix and investigations

CHAPTER 7

Writing about mathematics

Mathematics is a subject that people don't automatically associate with writing as it is seen as involving numbers and symbols. This chapter explores writing about mathematics and what this means for creative learning and creative teaching of mathematics. It obviously has links with literacy across the curriculum but it explores in more detail a different way of explaining and working with mathematics.

There are a number of aspects to writing in mathematics. The first is about communicating understanding of the mathematics undertaken. For young children this can involve writing about how they see calculations and give a clear indication of the associations they are making between mathematics and the real world.

Figures 7.1 and 7.2 show two different aspects of a young child's writing in mathematics. The first is in relation to the length of his name and the second example shows an example of noting what has been noticed in relation to a given task.

Why is it important for children to have opportunities to write in mathematics?

- It is important for children not to see mathematics as just about numbers and symbols but words can be used as well.
- Writing helps the clarity of oral explanation of ideas and processes.
- Writing can promote the clarity of thinking that is required when children are asked to explain their answers, particularly in test situations.
- Writing can promote discussion of what children have noticed and/or where they may have started from.
- Writing helps children to reflect upon their learning and reinforce the positive.
- Writing helps support different learning styles through the kinaesthetic act of writing, the visual impact of writing and the auditory approach when reading what has been written.

Figure 7.1 Writing about length

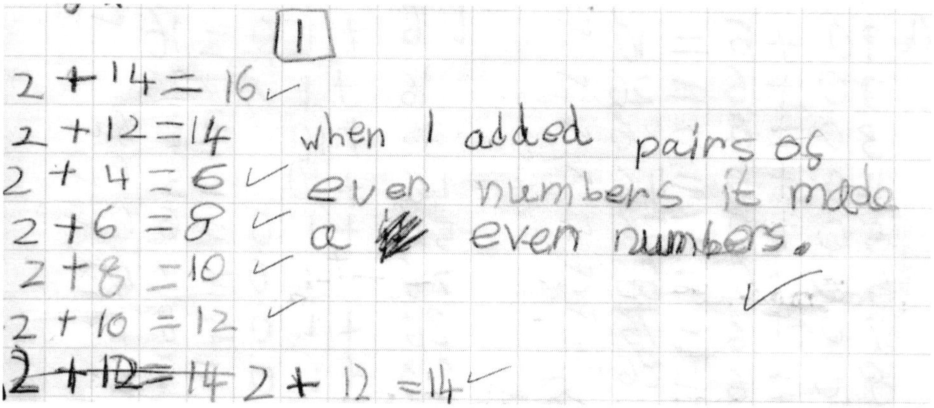

Figure 7.2 Writing about calculations

When considering what children should write about it is important to choose appropriate tasks. Children need to see that there is a purpose behind conveying the information in a written form. Most questions requiring a written response are given in a written form though they may have diagrams, graphs or other information to explore as well as the question.

Tasks and activities that promote writing may have the following characteristics:

- promote the need for discussion
- promote the need to write down instructions
- promote the need to write down a rationale for the approach taken to solve the task
- promote the need to justify the inclusion or exclusion of factors affecting the task
- promote the need to justify any answers given
- promote the need to communicate ideas
- promote the need to reflect upon the learning that has taken place.

The following are different examples of questions. As you read these, consider how they meet the characteristics outlined above.

Jo has written a number pattern that begins with 1, 3, 6, 10, 15. If she continues this pattern, what are the next four numbers in her pattern?
Or
Scientists have just discovered people on Neptune. There are 3 villages, 2 cities and 1 super city on Neptune. Table 7.1 the populations in 1994 and 1996.
List the places in order of increasing size in 1994 and 1996. In which year was the population of the planet greater? How did you decide?

Table 7.1 Population figures

	1994	1996
Eilosa	129	204
Vertu	308	292
Pridi	90	50
Dedrun	500	600
Antran	700	693
Maran	1200	1500

Or

In Figure 7.3 place the numbers 1 2 3 4 5 6 7 in the circles so each line adds up to 12.

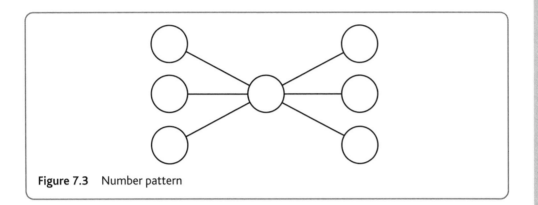

Figure 7.3 Number pattern

The last example here is typical of number based investigations and could be completed without any writing involved. The focus of writing here might be the strategies chosen in order to work out the answer to the problem. If the children then share their responses with another they can decide if there is more than one potential answer to the problem.

> **Task**
>
> Look at examples of different tasks available to you for the age group you teach. Do they promote writing about mathematics? Could they be adapted to promote writing about mathematics?

As this may be a very different approach for children they may need some support to work in this way. Being clear about expectations helps children as does the clarity of the initial introduction. The following are some suggestions.

Steps to support children working in this way

1. Ask the children to read the information carefully by themselves or read the information with them if this is appropriate.

2. Then ask one child within the group or class to read the question out aloud. Again this depends upon the reading ability and this may need to be a joint activity with the child and yourself.

3. Discuss with talk partners what they think the question(s) mean.

4. Discuss as a group/class the issues discussed in pairs. What did you notice about the graph? What patterns can you see? What questions will the information here allow you to answer? Can we predict what some of the answers might be from this information? Again, depending upon the age of the children, you may want them to write the questions themselves or for scribes to be available as a record of the discussion. In group work children could initially tape record their questions which could be transcribed later.

5. Also at this stage check understanding and correct use of vocabulary.

6. Do all children understand the context of any information?

7. Look carefully as a group/class at the kind of response that is expected or the kind of appropriate responses that would be expected from an open-ended task.

8. Give the children some time to work on their responses before bringing them back together with their draft ideas.

9. Take examples of children' responses and ensure they can justify their answers by giving a reasoned explanation. Questions like 'How did you know?'

10. Then give the group/class time to look at their draft responses and to write a precise and concise explanation using appropriate mathematical vocabulary. This drafting process can also be carried out as a larger group with an adult scribing the ideas.

11. Ask children to read aloud their responses and record a number of these on an IWB. Again, this may need more adult support with some groups of children.

12. Review the range of answers given and how they do or don't match the task.

13. Correct the responses where possible.

14. Ask the group/class to again review their responses to the questions and see if they can improve their original written explanations.

15. Finally share the improved responses.

The type of questions can be much more open and therefore require children to keep track of their thinking processes as they work.

Some examples of open-ended investigations follow:

- 2002 equals . . .
- Children are asked to investigate an aspect of palindromic numbers. They are to present an informative and interesting presentation summarising what they have found out. Palindromes are numbers or words that are the same forwards and backwards, e.g. 2002, 28 May 1982 – 28/5/82 and 35 + 53 = 88 are palindromes.

- Children are asked to write about mathematics and sport. What can they find out about the use of mathematics in sport which might include statistical information, the numbering of participants, timings and/or measuring.
- Calendar Numbers (see Figure 7.4):

Figure 7.4 Calendar

- select a Tuesday number — 8
- select a Thursday number — 17
- add them together — 25 – this is a Friday number

Add other Tuesday numbers to Thursday numbers. Do you always get a Friday number? Try some other days.

Young children and writing

For young children the writing might be about associations with a number as in Figure 7.5.

This writing does not have to be the children's but can be scribed for them after discussion of their ideas. They can use emergent writing at this age to begin to write their ideas about numbers. These ideas about number associations can be made into a book for display as discussed in Chapter 9.

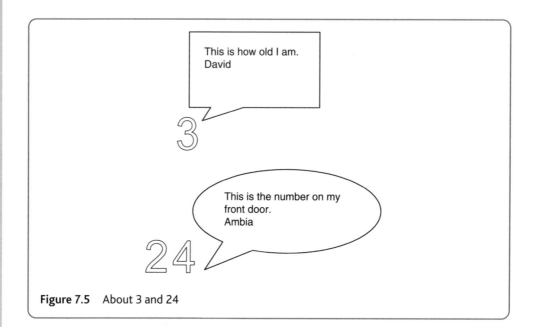

Figure 7.5 About 3 and 24

The affective domain

The other area of writing about mathematics is to write about feelings towards tasks given. Mathematics can be a challenging subject for many and there is a need for a release of some of the frustrations that can build up. One way is for children to have a mathematical journal in which they can write what they would like to at the end of a lesson. The following are some thoughts about how this can be supported within the class.

- Time needs to be set aside for review and writing within each lesson whether or not children actually write in each lesson.
- Children should be given the opportunity to write something everyday.
- Children should not necessarily be expected to write something everyday.
- Children should be encouraged to write in complete sentences which support literacy across the curriculum.
- Ideally, teachers should write with the children and share their work and ideas.
- Children should be given the opportunity to share their writing with others, pairs to begin with and then as confidence grows within a larger group or the class.
- Children should be given opportunities to share their journals with their parents and carers to promote discussion about learning mathematics outside school.

- Children should be encouraged to add to their entries outside school at weekends and during holidays. This will enable them to see the links with mathematics, their environment and activities outside school.
- Teachers should praise the children's work and use extracts as part of the classroom display.
- Children should be encouraged to include questions that they might not feel able to ask in the lesson.
- Children should be encouraged to find relationships between activities undertaken and make connections between the different aspects of mathematics. This links to the work of Askew et al. (1997) on the orientation of effective teachers of numeracy discussed in Chapter 2.
- Children should be encouraged to use their journal entries as revision notes in order to review topics, particularly if this includes procedures, processes and key facts.
- Children to see teachers and other adults writing and reflecting on the activities so it is not an activity that the children undertake on their own.

This may be something that you might want to try for a specific topic rather than for all lessons.

Task

Consider how you give opportunities for children to write in mathematics lesson. How could you introduce writing into your planning?

Other writing opportunities in mathematics

To create other opportunities for writing in mathematics the task designed needs to give children a purpose for writing. This also creates an opportunity for planning cross-curricular activities, for example with history, looking at the lives of notable mathematicians and writing biographical information about who they were, when and where they lived and what they were known for in the world of mathematics.

The web link www-groups.dcs.st-and.ac.uk/~history/BiogIndex.html provides biographical and other information about mathematicians. For example:

Pierre de Fermat
Born: 17 Aug 1601 in Beaumont-de-Lomagne, France
Died: 12 Jan 1665 in Castres, France

Pierre Fermat was the son of a wealthy leather merchant and he had a brother and two sisters. Although there is little evidence concerning his school education it must have been at the local Franciscan monastery. He attended the university of Toulouse before moving to Bordeaux in the second half of the 1620s. In Bordeaux he began his first serious mathematical researches. During this time he produced important work on maxima and minima. From Bordeaux, Fermat went to Orléans where he studied law at the university. He received a degree in civil law and he purchased the offices of councillor at the parliament in Toulouse. By 1631 Fermat was a lawyer and government official in Toulouse and because of the office he now held he became entitled to change his name from Pierre Fermat to Pierre de Fermat.

For the remainder of his life he lived in Toulouse but as well as working there he also worked in his home town of Beaumont-de-Lomagne and a nearby town of Castres, working as lawyer in the criminal courts and researching mathematics. Fermat was struck down by the plague and died in 1665.

The spiral (Figure 7.6) was discussed by Fermat in 1636.

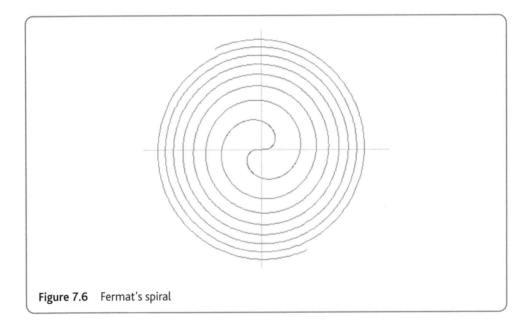

Figure 7.6   Fermat's spiral

Polar equation: $r^2 = a^2\,\theta$

For any given positive value of θ there are two corresponding values of r, one being the negative of the other. The resulting spiral will therefore be symmetrical about the line $y = -x$ as can be seen from the curve displayed above.

Although young children will not be able to engage in the mathematics that Fermat is describing here, images like this can be used to stimulate discussion and then writing about the image and the mathematician.

Task

Find out about a mathematician yourself. Who were they? When did they live? What specific aspects of mathematics did they work on? Can you find a mathematician that links to the topic you are teaching at the moment? What would you want the children to learn about this person? This links to the ideas about displaying information about mathematicians in Chapter 9.

Other links with history

There are two ways to link history with mathematics. The first is to link with topics in history and the other is to link directly with the history of mathematics.

Linking with history

English Heritage have produced materials which suggest that the historical environment is a rich primary source for investigations . . . 'bringing mathematics to the forefront of teachers' and children's thinking about the past and the physical evidence that survives from past times.' This physical environment can:

- help children come to terms with the passing of time, help put events and structures into perspective and in the appropriate time periods. Constructing time lines, it is possible to make links between history and mathematics to assist children's understanding.
- help explain how mathematics contributed to the development of an environment and how mathematics itself developed through the needs at the time. An example could be the measurement of right angles for building.
- help children record and represent previous environments. This offers opportunities for scaled drawings, marking out of sizes and shapes of environments to assist children to get a sense of places and situations. The size, shape and scale of walls to be breached as a foot soldier attacking a castle gives learners a greater understanding of the lives people led. One example of this

is the environment of a narrow boat and being able to appreciate that although the boats were large the space allocated to the living quarters for those living and working on board were cramped.

- help pupils to interpret and explain how the environment was used. Again, if we link this to the time of the narrow boats, the proportion or percentage of the boat used for cargo was much great than the living space.

Barker (2006) is a historian who has written a book about the Battle of Agincourt in which she details the preparations that Henry V made for his forces before battle. English bowmen were a key part of Henry's battle plans and they needed to be supplied with bows and arrows. The numbers of bows and arrows made are staggering. Stephen Seler, a London fletcher of the time, was commissioned to supply 12,000 arrows in one of many orders. These arrows had goose feather flights and Henry commanded his sheriffs to find him 1,190,000 feathers in 1418. He also commissioned the production of cannons at a cost of £107 10s 8d each. This was a costly campaign for Henry and the country. These represent a few of the interesting facts and figures that could be explored with children associated with this period of history. Alongside exploring the mathematics in history there are opportunities to learn about the lives of those involved during this period of history. One interesting fact about the armourers was that women were often employed as armourers, either as the wife of the armourer who took over running the armoury when her husband was away at war or sometimes in their own right. This shows quite a different perspective on women in history.

Ideas for using Agincourt as a starting point for mathematics:

- visiting a castle of the period
- measuring out the distances which arrows could be shot (between 150–240 yards)
- measuring arrows and lengths of bows
- hours of practise expected on the village green for all men between 16 and 60 years old
- visiting an archery range to gain a sense of the distances
- how prices compare with money now
- numbers of arrows an archer could shoot
- number of arrows the archers could/should carry
- the symmetry of fletchings needed for straight flight of arrows.

The illustration (Figure 7.7) taken from a child's history book.

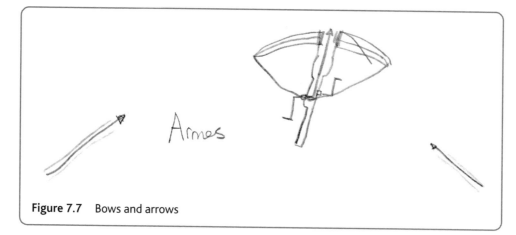

Figure 7.7   Bows and arrows

Figure 7.8 was also taken from a child's history book who was studying the French Revolution. It is a graph showing the number of people executed and which social

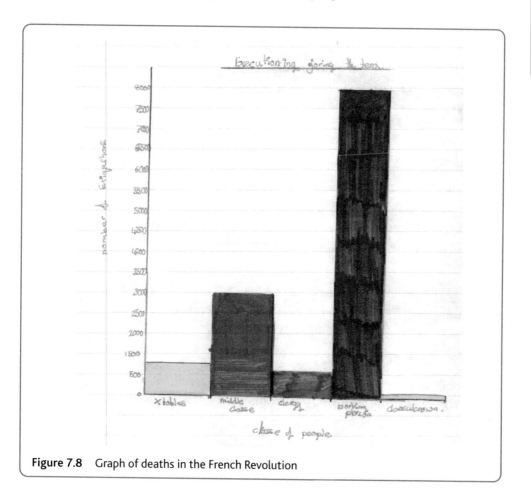

Figure 7.8   Graph of deaths in the French Revolution

groups they came from. This provides an interesting and gory starting point for some thinking about the data and what it means.

A secondary source of problems can be found in historical documents which can mean looking at mathematics problems in old texts. Alcuin's (800) 'propositio de campo et ovibus in eo locandis' is an example of a medieval problem set in *Problems for the Quickening of the Minds of the Young.* There is a field which is 200 feet long, 100 feet wide. I want to put sheep in it as follows: each sheep should have [an area] five feet long and four feet wide. How many sheep can be put in such a place?

Where would learners start with this problem? With young children it might be possible to make sheets of paper with sheep on which are five feet by four feet in size to cover a field marked out in the school grounds. The scale and sizes may be altered to accommodate the available space and age range.

For older children a scaled drawing of the field could be used to complete the same task. For this task, group writing may be a more effective tool than individual pieces of writing. The groups working on the task can use their written report as part of their feedback on the task and review of the learning that is taking place.

Task

Consider which areas of history are being taught. How could you use a primary source of information from the time to explore the mathematics involved?

History of mathematics

Avital (1995) suggests that history of mathematics is a valuable resource for teachers. The potential material available can be used with a wide range of age groups and can be differentiated to meet a variety of children's needs. Bidwell (1993) argues that the history of mathematics allows the following:

- communication about historical facts orally and/or in writing
- connecting mathematics to various cultures as well as other curriculum areas
- using history can substantially add to the learners value of mathematics.

It is important to appreciate that this is not about teaching children the history of mathematics but using the history of mathematics as a source of material to deliver creative teaching and facilitate learning.

Word problems

Word problems are used throughout the world as part of mathematics curricula. In relation to writing there are two issues: the first is reading someone else's writing and making sense of what is asked and the second is using the kinds of questions as a source of opportunities for writing.

Table 7.2 A sheet for solving a word problem

Word problem to be solved
Words in the problem I needed to check
Can I estimate what I think the answer will be
What kind of calculation is needed to solve the word problem
Clue word in the problem that shows what kind of a calculation is needed
Calculation
Check the calculation
Reread the problem and answer Is my answer sensible?
What have I learnt from answering this question?

The sheet above shows an example of the supportive structure that can be given to children to guide their writing in response to word problems. This acts in a similar way to a writing frame in literacy. Some of the sections focus on emphasising the vocabulary used and the specific meanings in mathematics.

Word problems can be used to start children writing sentence responses to questions posed. The important aspect of word problems is not just the completion of the mathematical parts of the task but making sure that the answer fits the context of the problem set, which can be seen in the guidance to return to the problem on completion of the calculation.

Children can also be asked to write word problems for each other or for younger children. In undertaking this kind of task they need to think about the clarity of their own writing. Below is a starting point for guidance that you might give to children in order to check the clarity.

Table 7.3   Writing a word problem

Is the context of the problem clear?
Does the problem make sense?
Does the problem indicate what answer is required?
Does the problem indicate if specific units are required in the answer?
Have I used appropriate vocabulary for the children who will answer the question?
Do I need to include a diagram, data or a picture?
What difference does a picture or other illustrations make to the clarity of the question?
Have I worked out the answer?
Can the question be answered?
Have I checked spelling and terms used in the question?
How will I finally present the question?
What have I learnt about word problems?

Task

Ask a group of children to either write questions in words for each other or for another different group of children. Try the guidance sheet above. How might you adapt this for your group of children? What do you think the children learnt about mathematics, writing about mathematics, and specifically about word problems?

Assessment and mathematical writing

One key area where children are expected to write, even if briefly, are in assessment tasks. It is important that children understand why the markers are interested in their thoughts expressed in writing within any assessment task. There are two functions, the first is so that aspects of working on the task can be credited and given marks and the other is to see what is actually happening when the children are working on the task. The first function is associated with summative assessment of learning tasks whereas the second function is seen as formative assessment or assessment for learning. This allows the teacher to plan the next steps in teaching and learning and to identify misconceptions to be addressed.

Figure 7.9 is from a National Curriculum test paper, QCA (2000), which shows clearly the relationship between the expectations of writing in assessment tasks for the end of KS2.

The issue here is the fact that most instructions related to writing in mathematics are 'copy' or 'complete' or 'how many?', therefore do not require children to explore their reasoning when they write. Many children can answer the first part of questions such as in this example but lose marks with the second part in supporting their reasoning.

One strategy to support children is to provide a writing frame (see Table 7.4) to structure their written work in mathematics as they develop their ideas. This can

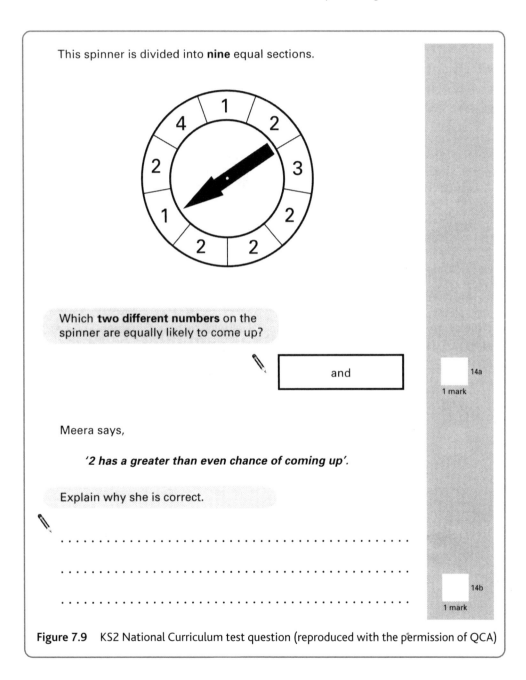

Figure 7.9   KS2 National Curriculum test question (reproduced with the permission of QCA)

support children's thinking and in turn support their skills in presenting their ideas orally.

This could be used with most of the examples of the problems in this chapter and could be used in conjunction with the games and other activities explored in Chapter 8.

Table 7.4 A writing frame

The activity/task I have been given is . . .
What I have to find out is . . .
I have noticed . . .
I think . . .
The reason I think this is . . .
Another thing I have noticed is . . .
I have learnt . . . for next time

This chapter has introduced some aspects of writing about mathematics writing and has shown how this might be developed for children of all ages. Again, this is intended as a starting point for developing aspects of practice in areas that you may not have considered.

CHAPTER 8

Games and other similar activities

This chapter looks at games and other activities as a starting point for creative learning and teaching of mathematics. The starting point for these games is not a published scheme of mathematical games or a concentration on board games. Here the focus is again on looking at other activities you may already include in your teaching and the children's learning but not necessarily for mathematics.

Why use games in learning and teaching mathematics?

- Games can lower the feelings of failing
- Games can encourage successful learning and increase self-esteem
- Games can help children and adults make connections between aspects of mathematics
- Games can foster a sense of engagement through taking part in the activity
- Games can enable links with learning rules, roles within games as well as specific mathematics
- Games can encourage mathematical discussion between children and with adults
- Games can help support the introduction of new areas and ideas
- Games can help reinforce knowledge in different ways
- Games can support different learning styles by providing a different format for similar activities
- Games can provide an opportunity to move around whilst learning mathematics
- Games can be fun.

Making choices about games to use with children

Choosing a game need not be a difficult issue. Adapting games that are played in other areas of the curriculum can be a good starting point. One such example is the game sometimes called fruit salad. This is a game usually played with children sitting in a circle in a large space like a hall, all facing into the centre of the circle. In the original version the children are labelled as apple, orange, pear and banana, for example. The game continues with someone calling out a fruit and then all those who have been labelled as that fruit get up and run around the outside of the circle in one direction until they reach their original position. The last person returning is out and remains sitting in the circle whilst the others run around. The call of fruit salad requires everyone to get up and run altogether. A maths version of this game can be played with children being given a number and then the calls depending upon age of the children can be:

- odd numbers
- even numbers
- numbers under ten
- numbers more than ten
- numbers between three and nine
- multiples of a number – two, five
- divisible by a number
- and to get everyone up calling all numbers or a similar phrase.

This game allows children to think about numbers in a fun and different way. When playing the game, children are quick to tell others in the class to run if they have worked out that a number is included in the parameters of the call.

There can be huge variations in the numbers used for this. For younger children just numbering them 1–5 in a repeating pattern may enable them to think about appropriate questions. Whereas for Y6 the numbers may be fractions or decimals or may not start at 1 to add a level of challenge and enable the game to be played more than once without children feeling that they have played this before. By keeping the rules and the format of the game the same it allows a sense of security for children as they don't have to think about the rules and can concentrate on the numbers being used. Shapes could also be used if the children are given cards with pictures of the shapes on to focus their attention on the properties of the shapes.

Task

Find a physical game and consider how it could be adapted to emphasise an aspect of mathematics. Try to choose a game with rules with which the children are familiar as this makes it easier for everyone involved to concentrate on the mathematical aspects rather than rules.

Guess who I am?

Most teachers include some guessing games in their teaching and here is just one example of how these kinds of activities may be used in mathematics. 'Guess who I am?' is a game which in the first version involves pairs of children who have a number or a shape placed on their forehead using a Post-it sticker. They then compete against each other to guess what they have on their heads by taking it in turn to ask questions of their partner. I may have an 8 on my forehead and so may ask questions like: am I bigger than ten or am I an even number? The partner may only answer yes or no to the questions. As soon as one of the pair thinks they know what number they are they can offer a guess.

This may look ideal but you may feel your class couldn't play this in pairs. They may need to be introduced to and play the game a number of times with a larger group to gain the idea before working with a partner. With a whole class this can be played with one person with a number or shape on their forehead asking questions of the whole class or it could be played with a small group competing against each other in front of the class asking the questions. An alternative strategy is for a child to choose a number and the rest of the class asking questions of the individual to guess which number or shape they have chosen.

With younger children being able to see the number or the shape can help them to ask or answer questions as they have the stimulus of the item. Limiting the number, for example, that could be the answer can assist children think about the particular properties, such as, even. Children could have a board each with numbers 0–20 on and be able to cross off numbers with a marker if they have decided that number is not the one being described until they only have one left. This is similar to the guess who game involving faces where one is chosen that each player must guess by eliminating those who don't match the criteria given.

Task

Try a version of 'guess who or what I am' that is most appropriate for the age group in your teaching. What differences did you notice about children's language? What do you notice about their involvement in the activity?

Adapting initial ideas

From ideas that you may read about or see others using it is possible to begin the creative teaching process by adapting the idea to match the needs of the children with which you work. The following example does just that to show the process that is possible.

What is missing?

Another adaptation of the 'guess who I am' game is to give small groups of children a bag with numbers on cards inside but with one of the sequence missing and for the group to work out which number is missing and then present their answer to the rest of the class. This promotes discussion between members of the group and again adds interest. Teams of children gain a point for each correct answer whilst additional points can be given for the explanations. For some children the sequence might be 1, 2, –, 4, 5 with the missing number being 3 but it could equally well be 27, –, 45, 54 with the missing number being 36 or ¼, –, ¾, 1 where the missing number is a ½. Sequences could include decimals and percentages or patterns based upon other rules to give greater challenges. The time to solve the game problems might also need to be increased along with the challenge, if appropriate.

Historical sources of logic problems and games

Historical documents can be an interesting source of problems that can be used as a starting point for children to work on. These are, in the main, specific problems that have a specific outcome to answer the question. They can often be simplified to an algebraic formula. The examples here are not chosen for that reason but to show what is a potential starting point for mathematical thinking and mathematical discussion. There are some issues about using historical activities as the language used and the situations can now be seen as stereotyping. Depending upon individual teachers' confidence this may be an area that can be discussed when presenting the activity. Language and views of different situations have changed and that is an important aspect of using historical sources. When you choose activities these are issues that you need to bear in mind.

The river-crossing problem

This problem is attributed to Alcuin (800) 'propositio de homine et capra et lupo' but there are a wide range of these involving different items but the same premise behind the problem. The problem is sometimes seen as the problem of three jealous husbands (each of whom won't let another man be alone with his wife) and the problem of 'the two adults and two children where the children weigh half as much as the adults. Other modifications include the addition of more people, an island in the centre, and a bigger boat. Problems similar to the wolf–goat–cabbage problem have appeared in a variety of cultures.

> A certain man needed to take a wolf, a she-goat and a load of cabbage across a river. However, he could only find a boat which would carry two of these 'at a time'. Thus, what rule did he employ so as to get all of them across unharmed?

Unfortunately the man dare not leave the wolf alone with the goat or the goat alone with the cabbage for the wolf would eat the goat and the goat would eat the cabbage.

The solution to this problem is for the man to take the goat across leaving the cabbage and the wolf together. Then on the next trip he picks up the cabbage and returns with the cabbage swapping the cabbage and the goat over. He then returns to the wolf and swaps the goat and the wolf to take the wolf to join the cabbage. His final trip means he collects the goat to complete the task of bringing them all safely across the river.

This kind of problem is one that can be accessed by children in reception. In one class the children were introduced to the problem in groups with a boat, a man, a wolf and a goat as cut-outs that they could move about. This is not real problem solving as the problem was posed by the teacher and there is only one solution. Children initially always come up with their own innovative responses. At first there were ones such as 'I'd throw the cabbage across the river' or 'the wolf could swim across' or 'he should make the goat swim and he could encourage him by having the cabbage on a string behind the boat, that way the wolf and the man could be in the boat' or 'they walk down the path to find a bridge.' These initial responses show that the children are engaging with the story and beginning to think of solutions. Having explained again that the boat is the only means of getting across the river the group then started to think carefully about the problem. They delighted in telling each other when one of the items would be eaten. 'I suggest he throws the cabbage across the river.' This starting point works on children's logic thinking, an area that will support their investigative skills and algebraic thinking.

Gradually they arrived at a solution using the cut-outs and a paper river to cross. They moved on to having a go at a computer programme that had a similar problem of two women and two girls crossing the river. The boat in this case can either hold one woman or two girls but no other combinations. Some of the groups in the class moved on to make their own versions of the problem involving more animals or totally different ones. Some of the children recorded the steps in the problem with a mixture of pictures and initial letters as their symbols for the objects. So 'm' became man, 'c' became cabbage, 'w' became wolf and 'g' became goat. A good link to the need to teach phonics to this age group!

This problem was also tried with a class of Y2/3 children using it to fit into a topic about the weather and temperature. In this case the version involved an Inuit, an arctic hare, an arctic fox and a clump of tundra grass that were crossing a gap in the ice in a kayak. The recording from this class became more detailed with diagrams including symbols to explain the moves. The most able were able to generalise the moves to different situations. An alternative approach could be to get groups to act out the problem with one member of the group directing the others acting the parts. Everyone has on opportunity to contribute to the discussion and remind the director if they are in a position to eat something, e.g. the goat left with the cabbage. This is something that children like doing with each other and it also makes the learning experience memorable for all participants.

The handshakes problem

Again this is a well-known problem. In this case the problem was introduced to children as the king's party where everyone is asked to shake hands with everyone else as they arrive. (They don't shake hands with themselves.) How many handshakes will there be as each person arrives?

The following examples show some Y3 children's recording of this problem.

The first example shows a girl who chose to respond to the problem in writing, as seen in Figure 8.1, which links to the content of Chapter 7 of this book.

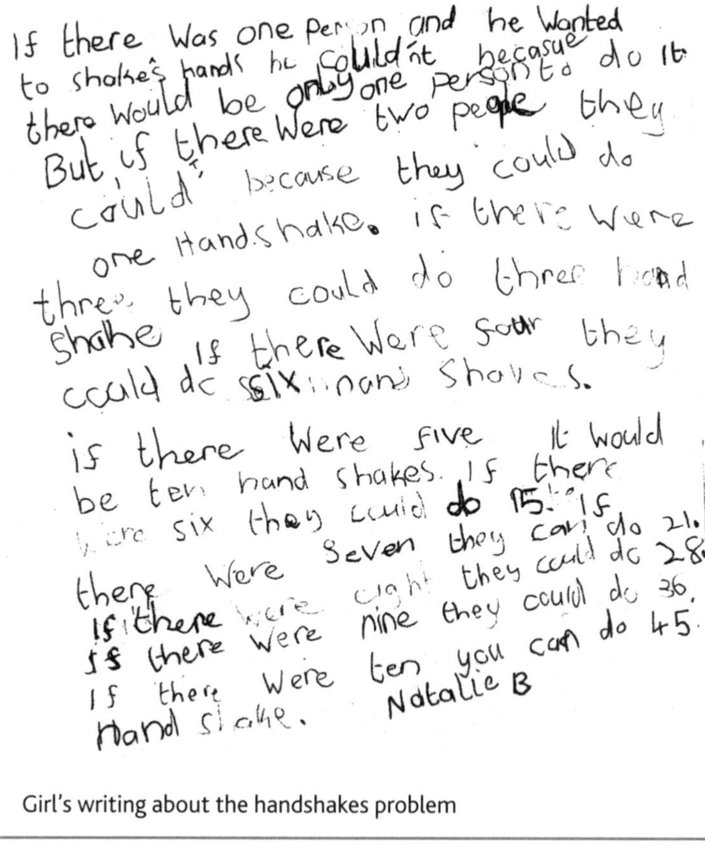

If there Was one person and he Wanted to shake's hands he could'nt becasue there would be only one person to do it. But if there were two people they could because they could do one Handshake. if there were three they could do three hand shake if there were four they could do six hand shakes.

is there Were five it would be ten hand shakes. If there were six they could do 15. If there Were Seven they can do 21. If there were eight they could do 28. If there were nine they could do 36. If there were ten you can do 45. Hand shake.

Natalie B

Figure 8.1 Girl's writing about the handshakes problem

The second example of responses to the problem shows two diagrammatic approaches where the children have drawn the handshakes across between the people (see Figure 8.2). The child on the right seems to have become confused after working out the number of handshakes for five people and has given up the recording for six or more people.

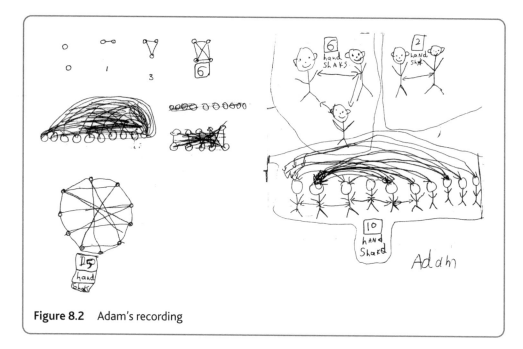

Figure 8.2 Adam's recording

The next two examples show a move towards a symbolic representation of people with one of the examples exploring whether the number of handshakes was different if there was a person standing in the middle of the group (Figure 8.3).

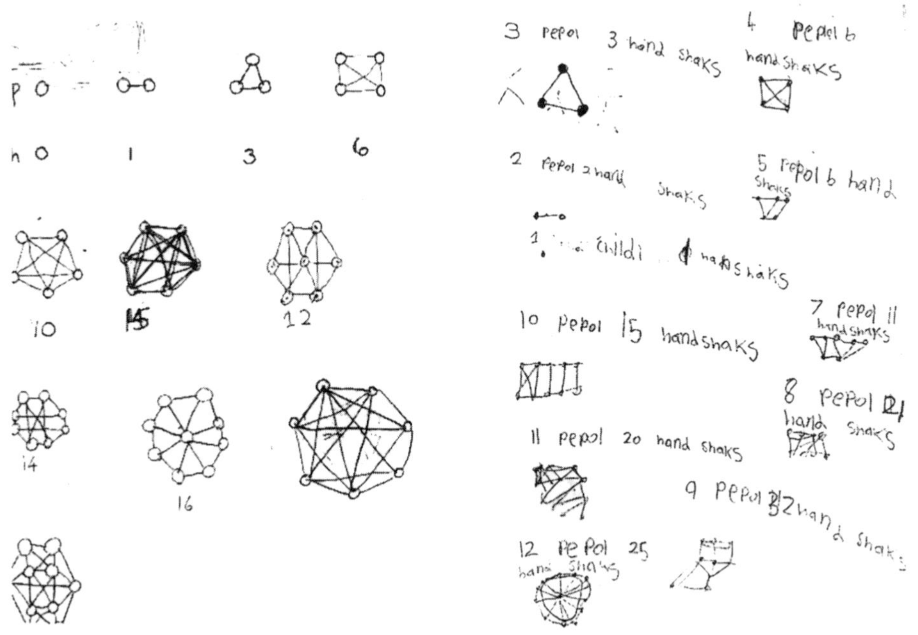

Figure 8.3 Recording the handshakes problem

The Tower of Hanoi

The Tower of Hanoi puzzle was invented by the French mathematician Edouard Lucas in 1883. The problem starts with a tower of eight disks, initially stacked in increasing size on one of three pegs. The objective is to transfer the entire tower to one of the other pegs, moving only one disk at a time and never a larger one onto a smaller.

Josephus Flavius game

Josephus Flavius was a famous Jewish historian of the first century at the time of the Second Temple destruction. During the Jewish-Roman war he got trapped in a cave with a group of 40 soldiers surrounded by Romans. The legend has it that preferring suicide to capture, the Jews decided to form a circle and, proceeding around it, to kill every third remaining person until no one was left. Josephus, not keen to die, quickly found the safe spot in the circle and thus stayed alive. The purpose of the game, of course, is to stay alive by choosing the right spot. Again, there are a number of versions of this problem; this puts different groups together, pitting them against each other. This problem offers an ideal opportunity to consider ethics with children and as such is more suitable for older children. This is an ideal problem to use people as the model and again encourages movement as part of visualisation in mathematics.

> *Task*
>
> Find a problem to try out with your learners from a historical source. What kinds of mathematics skills do you think these enabled children to work on by presenting activities in this way? Which learning styles do you think this focused on?

Using well-known games

Dominoes

Dominoes are seen as an old fashioned resource but they can be used as games in a number of different ways. Simple matching of dominoes is still used in many infant classes. The game of fives and threes still played in pubs and clubs is an excellent game to promote knowledge of multiples of particularly fives and threes. It is usually played with a cribbage pegboard to score but can be played with score-keeping on a piece of paper. The idea behind the game is that you only score if the sum of the ends of the string of dominoes is a multiple of three or five and if you get a total that is both a multiple of five and three then there is a double score. For example, if the ends equal 5 the score is 1, if the ends equal 6 the score is two, if the score is 15 with a double five at one end and a single five at the other the score is 8 as $5 \times 3 = 15$ and $5 \times 3 = 15$. The object of the game is to score as many times as you can whilst stopping your opponent from scoring.

Dominoes can also be the basis of adapting activities that make mathematics lessons active. Variations on loop cards, for example find the partner, where all the children have a card and they have a set time in which to find the person who has the card that matches theirs or complements theirs. Some examples are 7 matches with all the cards are complements of 10 or $4 + 5 = 9$ matches $9 - 5 = 4$. Dominoes can be made to reinforce the topic being taught, e.g. shapes, and Figure 8.4 shows examples of the dominoes.

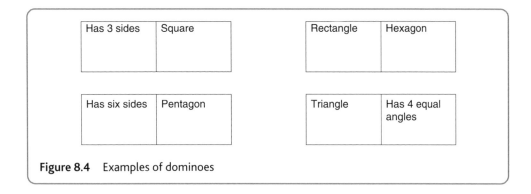

Figure 8.4 Examples of dominoes

These can be resources that the adults make but they can also be resources that the children can make and trial by playing the game to make sure that the matches work for the whole set of dominoes made.

Games of routes using mazes

This is a game-like format for practising calculations. The children find the route from the start to the finish of the maze and carry out the calculations required as they move. An example of a maze can be seen in Figure 8.5.

Questions can be asked of children to find the route from the top to the bottom that will produce the biggest number or the smallest number. The numbers on each of the parts of the route can be altered to provide different levels of challenge for different ages and abilities. Children can make their own route problems for others to try as well as designing their own mazes with accurate measurement of each pathway.

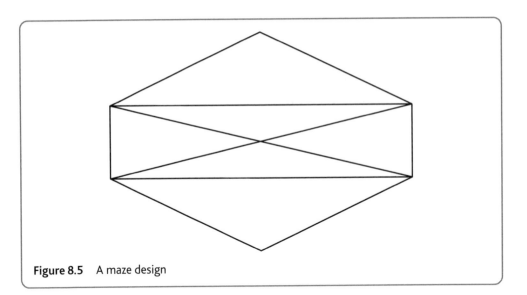

Figure 8.5 A maze design

Darts

Although it would not be sensible to suggest that darts with sharp points are used in the classroom, sets with magnets or Velcro fastenings can be used safely. Dartboards also don't need to be hanging on the wall but can be on the floor and the dart thrower be aiming darts or substitute darts onto a dartboard. A dartboard on the floor with bean bags to throw onto the face to score can be a substitute. This can be used in a wide variety of ways. For reinforcement of subtraction, subtract the score from 301 or 501 with the winner being the first who reaches zero. Other ideas can be to add the scores until a given score is reached. Two darts or bean bags can be thrown and the two numbers score can be multiplied. All these activities can be carried out on a 'normal' dartboard. The dartboard base can be altered to meet the needs of the children and the numbers that are emphasised.

Other games that could be used as the basis for activities for mathematics teaching and learning are tiddlywinks, Connect Four and hopscotch.

> *Task*
> Look carefully at the games that are in your classroom/nursery/school. Don't forget to also look at the games in the playground that could be used outside so you are not just thinking about inside activities. How might one of these games be used to create an opportunity for the teaching and learning of mathematics? Try the game out with children and evaluate the activity in relation to children's learning and the opportunities to focus on mathematics as part of the game.

Resources for games development

Collecting boards from discarded games as well as small items to act as counters for moving around the boards are essential for beginning to think about a range of resources for children to make their own games. In order that children can produce effective and high quality games they need access to a wide range of resources. The range is important to assist their creativity and offer ideas for the design of games. At a simple level this can be taking an existing board from a game and adding mathematics questions to a set of cards that are picked up at specific points on the board.

Using the format from current popular game show television programmes

One approach to developing creative teaching and learning is to use the current ideas and formats from popular television programmes as the basis of activities in the classroom. An example of this is *Who wants to be a millionaire?* When questions are asked children can use the rules from the programme when children are offered four different possible answers to a question:

- ask (phone) a friend
- ask (the audience) the rest of the team or class
- 50 : 50

And before an answer is accepted 'Is that your final answer?'

This can be used for either individuals or a team in the classroom. If your setting or school has the technology to link up individuals with a participant/personal response system (PRS) to a display then they can each answer the question. The results can be displayed for the whole class to discuss. The questions set would obviously depend upon the age of the children and so this format is very flexible.

Mastermind

Mastermind is another game format that could be considered for mathematics. The television version includes two rounds of questions, one on a chosen specialist subject and the second of general knowledge questions. Children could choose to spend time researching their specialist subject, which might be triangles as an example, and then answer as many questions about triangles for a minute or the limit could be a bank of 10 questions. The second round of questions could then be general mathematics questions. This game format offers children choice and encourages independent personalised learning especially for their specialist subject. The children could either be answering questions individually or they could work within teams in the class. The actual format developed will be dependant on the children's age and previous knowledge and experiences. If a time limit is used to answer questions this could be displayed using a counter program on the IWB with a chosen noise to end the round of the game.

Other television formats that could be used are:

- *Weakest Link* (the opportunity to vote off those who might normally win)
- *Deal or No Deal* (the numbers in the boxes could be changed and you might ask a colleague to be the banker with offers, who could phone into the classroom maybe using a mobile phone).

Task

Consider a current popular television programme that has a format you could use as part of the teaching and learning for mathematics. Could you use the chosen format for a starter for a lesson or a review activity?

The chapter has looked at a small number of potential ideas for using games and other activities as a starting point for developing creative learning and teaching in mathematics. The main focus has been for the adults to suggest the starting points to interest children but by listening to children they will be a real source of other ideas that could be developed.

CHAPTER 9

Display and the classroom environment

This chapter looks at display and the classroom which are important elements in creating an environment which supports both creative teaching and learning. The majority of classrooms have lively displays of children's work. Mathematics, however, is often last on the list for display. Although in many schools/settings this has become a task undertaken by teaching assistants rather than teachers, planning the displays should still be part of the teacher's role to create this stimulating environment for the learners including the adults. This chapter looks at why display of mathematics is important for developing children's creative thinking skills.

> **Task**
>
> Take a walk around the place you work and look for images of mathematics that are already on display. You are looking for two different forms of images, those that show children's work or information about mathematics and images that may be used for teaching, e.g. number lines or squares. These all help to convey images of mathematics. Do these suggest to the people viewing these displays that mathematics can be creative?

You may have found some images for teaching purposes but in terms of other images there may not be much around. You may have seen displays of handling data, tessellations and the odd pieces of shapes stuck to the wall. You may also have seen some number lines and squares. If you are working in the Early Years at what point do the numbers stop? Is it 10, 20 or further?

In her biography, the Russian mathematician Sofia Kovalevskaya has a message for all those teaching mathematics. She claims to have studied her father's old calculus notes that were papered on her nursery wall in replacement for a shortage of wallpaper. As a result of this experience she said that when she met the mathematics she had been looking at in the nursery in her studies it was like meeting old friends.

We can encourage our learners to think creatively about mathematics by 'mathematising' the learning environment. Children should have access to a wide range of resources within the environment and have displayed materials that are thought-provoking in relation to mathematics. A simple question like 'What is the biggest number you know?' can result in children talking to each other about how large a number they can count to, they can write or they can read.

Task

Consider the place of display in your setting/school.

Why are the specific materials being displayed?

- to promote the area of the curriculum
- to celebrate children's achievements
- to stimulate interest
- to show care and interest in children's work – valuing what they do
- to show the range of work achieved across a class or age range or the school
- to promote the setting/school
- as part of event(s) associated with the curriculum area
- to show cross-curricular links, e.g. art and mathematics, ICT and mathematics.

Where is material displayed?

- class
- corridor
- hall
- outside setting/school.

Who will be looking at the display?

- parents/carers
- colleagues
- children
- governors/inspectors/visitors.

Is the display going to be used for teaching purposes? The display may form part of the teaching but also serve as a record of work completed and this will change the form and design of the display. What form of display would be most appropriate for this material? Is the display to go up altogether or is it a display that will be added to over time? This may be a function of the display's purpose.

Making the most of display is an important part of any planning. In mathematics this has been an under-utilised aspect of teaching the subject. You may have seen displays of tessellation and/or handling data but perhaps little else mathematical. Think carefully as you plan activities for mathematics to include those it would be possible to display.

Display conveys messages to children, parents and others about values and the worth of specific activities. In the eyes of the children, displaying work reinforces the value you place on it. It shows you care about their work. When displaying mathematics you need to make decisions about whether or not everyone's work is displayed. This is particularly important if work is marked and negative comparisons might be made by children, parents or others. Mathematics is often completed in books and so much of the work recorded is never displayed. What image of mathematics does this convey to children?

Vary the types of display in the classroom but think about the difficulties that some forms can cause. For instance, having lots of items hanging from the ceiling low enough so that children can read them may look nice but can result in limited freedom of movement for the adults in the room. Try grouping hanging displays together away from doors or windows. Displays can also be used to denote different areas of the classroom or where the equipment for mathematics is stored. The room you are working in may have limited display space in which case you need to think about how else to offer children and others opportunities to peruse samples of work.

You don't have be an artist to produce good display as it is best when the children's work is obviously theirs and not a teacher's! Mounting work can make small drawings or recordings look much better. You do need to be good with glue and a cutter in order to get the mounting right.

It is also worth involving the children in the process of completing the display however small that involvement is with small children. You will also need to decide on the overall finished effect you are trying to create. The look of children's work can be enhanced by mounting well but the finished product should still look like a child's work.

Equipment

- a good set of numbers and letters stencils are useful
- access to a computer with a colour printer for printing different style lettering
- good scissors and pinking shears for different edgings
- a good set of different thickness pens (including gold and silver) – not ones used by children for colouring
- a clean metre ruler
- stamps of coins or numbers which can be used to create borders

- discarded wrapping paper, again for part of borders or corner interest
- a collection of interesting material for draping
- a sharp knife for cutting large rolls of paper at the edge of boards
- a staple gun for use after positioning with drawing pins.

Backgrounds on boards

The background of a board can be any of the following:

- a single colour
- two tones of the same colour either in a checker board pattern or one tone with a few of the other tone at angles over the top
- old wallpaper
- wrapping paper
- a single colour with a silhouette of an item for the area of focus – for example a set of scales for a background of a display on weight.

Borders

Borders are a neat way of finishing a board and can be:

- a single thin border
- a double border in contrasting colours to the background
- a single or double border in a different tone of the colour of the background
- a border of items associated with the theme of the display – e.g. coins for a money display
- the border items can be 3-D like boxes from sweets placed at intervals around the border when the display is of an investigation of costs of sweets in different packaging or is about the nets to create 3-D shapes.

Labelling

This can be:

- computer printed
- handwritten

- in speech bubbles
- stencilled
- written by children
- statements
- questions.

Display as a stimulus

This can be for setting up a classroom at the beginning of the year/term or it could be as the starting point for discussion of a particular topic in mathematics.

Display is part of creating a stimulating environment for learning; what is displayed for pupils to look at and use is of key importance. As a new teacher, by putting some display in the classroom you can begin to show your presence and children do notice. The same is true for an established teacher setting up a class for a new group of children. When starting a classroom from scratch, without any children's work to display, then the items put up on the walls or left out for the children to look at and explore could reflect the themes of the work planned and give children an indication of the aspects they will be learning about.

Ideas for the new room

Posters related to the theme can be a good starting point, for example pictures up on the walls showing the changes in the environment due the seasons. A poster of vocabulary associated with say division; division, share, and divide, for example, which can be drawn from the vocabulary materials from the NNS/PNS.

A display of shapes and other interesting items can be left on a low table for children to handle and look at, including hand lenses or magnifiers which encourage children to look more closely where appropriate. You can follow this up with actually teaching the children how to use these pieces of equipment in the first few days to reinforce the skills and again encourage interaction with the display.

An empty number spider as the starting point for a lesson can be prepared ahead of the lesson. This can be added to as the lesson progresses for instant display and feedback for the children about their responses.

A 100 square can be used as a starting point for looking at routes and patterns that might be useful for calculation or investigating.

Children often need to be directed to the mathematics in a display and the aspects of mathematics you can see in a picture might not be apparent to a child. This can be emphasised through labelling, arrows or directing the children to the display during the teaching time. Try to engage children with what is mathematical by asking specific questions within the display. How many rectangles can you see? Is the man twice as high as the dog or is he three times as high? Name all the different shapes you can find. If you do not know the names, how can you describe them to your teacher so he/she can tell you the names? Or offering questions and answer routes from a shape to its name like a flow diagram, which could be three dimensional with cord between the questions and answers to form an interactive display.

Display as part of an activity or lesson

Display can be used as the basis of an activity itself, as part of an interactive display and mathematics lends itself to being more than a static display. It could be the first part of a large display as there is often an assumption that a display has to be finished and be put up in one go.

Where to get ideas from

Look out for good display for potential ideas and jot down sketches and ideas from effective displays you see in schools, books and centres so that you build up a file of ideas on which you can draw. Be warned that good display takes as much preparation time as teaching itself but it is well worth the effort. Shop windows can give ideas for themes for display.

You may have good ideas for other areas of the curriculum but find ideas more limited for mathematics. If this is the case think about what makes a good display. How is your eye drawn to the items? What kinds of borders can be eye-catching?

An example of something different

'People mathematics' activities photographed could be displayed on a background with 'dollies' cut from paper around the edge as the border. A good display for weight, for example, might involve a series of washing lines. There was a 10 gram line, a 100 gram line and a 100 line. Pupils are invited to take a transparent plastic bag and fill it with as many of an object as necessary to give the desired weight or to count 100 of them into a bag. The visual impact of seeing 100 counters and 100 sheets of paper as having sameness is very powerful and can lead to valuable discussion.

A measurement display in a ks2 class may start with the vocabulary associated with measures. A board could be prepared ahead of time with a border using either old tape measures or strips of paper marked to look like tape measures. Children could then be invited to add words to the board. Pre-cutting the paper should ensure the size of the labels but children may need assistance in writing large enough for others to read.

Reinforcement

Picking up on other things you might use in the classroom – an example of this is the use of TV or video programmes. The Megamaths Multiplication video has two characters that are set each side of the entrance to a castle. If you take the idea from the programme you could set up an entrance on a board to reinforce the table being learnt at the time. The border could be a castellation design in one colour against a contrasting colour. The final touch would be the characters from the programme each side. You don't have to be an artist – get the children to draw the characters and add their work to the display.

Mobiles and use of hangers

A mobile of shapes is an obvious example that you may be familiar with, what about a mobile of number bonds or a mobile for a multiplication table? Hangers with socks or gloves grouped in multiples can support multiplication as well.

Display for teaching number

With the introduction of the National Numeracy Strategy teachers have been concerned about the materials to support the teaching and learning of number.

Number lines and tracks

Number lines (see Figure 9.1) are where the number is above or below the lines like a ruler.

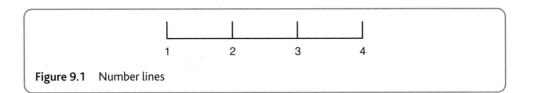

Figure 9.1 Number lines

Number tracks (see Figure 9.2) have the numbers in the spaces between the lines.

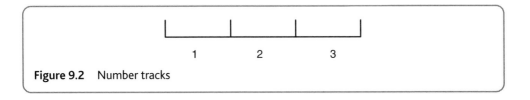

Figure 9.2 Number tracks

When using a track the focus is on the jump between the numbers (see Figure 9.3).

These can prove difficult to include in many classes as what is really required is a long straight wall with ideally somewhere at child height to fix the line.

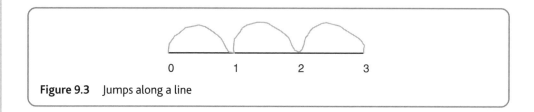

Figure 9.3 Jumps along a line

If possible, a useful way to display a number line is to fix the bottom of it to the wall leaving the top loose. This means you can fix pegs to the top which is particularly useful for working on difference.

If your room does not have a continuous wall space it is possible to consider different approaches to using a line or track. If you have an old teacher's breakthrough stand you can put a line/track into the stand to use with a group though it may not be big enough to be seen by the whole class at once. An alternative is to make a wooden stand to fix a line to which can be left standing on the floor when not in use.

100 squares

Again a large space is needed for the square if it is to become a permanent fixture. Squares which have detachable numbers are useful as a teaching device. An example of how to use a square like this can be seen on the Hamilton Project video. Either questions can be displayed alongside the 100 square or they can be posed orally by the teacher.

To produce a fully Velcroed 100 square can be a lengthy undertaking. You also need to be careful about the choice of glue as Velcro requires stronger glue, even to attach it to card. (You spent time gluing twice as the first time the glue wasn't strong enough to hold the Velcro and keep it attached for children to pull the squares off and on!!) If you want children to use the square then positioning it in the class may mean that you are looking at displaying it where you haven't got display boards. You may have a small easel or blackboard to which you could attach a square. An alternative is to have the square hung up but when you wish to use it for teaching arrange to move it to a table top. In order that the square will stand up you will need to attach a form of stand to the original square (see Figure 9.4).

Another alternative is to have a hanging form of the 100 square which could be tied up out of the way when not in use. This is probably an easier suggestion for an older school building or a room with lower ceilings.

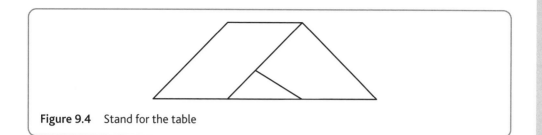

Figure 9.4   Stand for the table

Number spiders

If the answer is 24 what is the question?

Calculations could be placed at each end of the lines which might be drawn or made from string or ribbon. Alternatively, several of these could form a small display with the calculations around the outside and the answer covered. This could be a good starting point for a main activity. What numbers could the middle one be? Can you estimate the size of the number without working it out first? If I think I know the answer which calculation will I use to test it out on?

Calendars

Large calendars can be used for teaching. Some schools make calendars and an enlarged version may be part of a display in a central area in the school. Alternatively, a number of print programmes for computers allow you to create your own pages of a calendar month by month that may be part of a display or a central item.

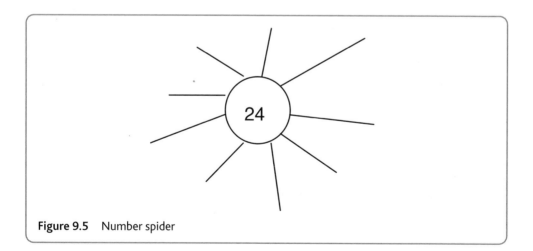

Figure 9.5   Number spider

Number collections

For young children collections of sets of seven objects to reinforce the concept of seven or any other number can support their development of number. For KS2 collections of odd numbers or prime numbers or percentages could be used to stimulate exploration and discussion. Other collections might include house numbers which the children can order or sort and explain their rationale for particular responses. Although these are all collections of number areas, other aspects of mathematics can be considered, for example collections of how data is handled in the media for discussion and interpretation.

Washing lines

A big difficulty of washing lines is that ideally they need to be available all the time, particularly for young children to play with outside the teaching time; however, this creates problems in many classrooms. For the washing line to be low enough for children to reach means that it presents a potential hazard for adults. Some teachers use washing lines across the black or white board for teaching. This means the line has to be taken down when the mathematics session has finished and it cannot be explored at other times by the children. Alternative strategies include stringing a washing line across a corner of a large classroom or using old sports posts between which to hang the line. The latter can be moved out of the way when not being used but also have the advantage of existing stable bases which will not fall over if knocked in a busy classroom.

Felt walls

Felt walls to which children can stick objects, words, numbers and pictures using Velcro can be a very versatile resource. This is nice idea for young children which we originally saw used throughout a Bradford school to support teaching and learning across the curriculum. If there is space put a felt wall near the carpet area. This felt wall is then used to place cards with numerals, dots, number names for ordering, for example. This arrangement could also be used for making repeating patterns of shapes as it is not just a resource for teaching and learning about number aspects of mathematics. In Early Years classes the resources can be left for the children to explore in free-play situations as well as 'taught' sessions encouraging them to engage with the materials and the ideas.

Forms of display

Display space may be at a premium so you might like to consider the following suggestions for other ways of displaying mathematics material.

Books

Making books is an obvious solution as they can hold large amounts of written work, photographs and other records of activities. Books can also be in concertina or zigzag format.

Displays around school and the role of the co-ordinator or curriculum leader or teaching and learning manager

> ### Task
>
> Who has responsibility for display in classrooms and around school? Is there a plan of what should be displayed and why?

Displays can raise the awareness of mathematics for pupils and for other teachers. As a co-ordinator, either for mathematics or for teaching and learning across the school, you should be a trendsetter with the displays of mathematics in your classroom. Display anywhere in the school can assist in raising the awareness of mathematics not just inside the school but for parents and other visitors. The progression of mathematics work across the age range of the school, for example in a specific aspect of mathematics, could be displayed in a prominent place in the school to attract prospective parents and even impress inspectors. With the Primary National Strategy, the responsibilities in some schools are shifting, with new emphases on cross-curricular working. A teacher with this responsibility also has to look at mathematics across the curriculum and promote teaching and learning throughout the school.

Display around the school is one opportunity to work with a co-ordinator of a different subject if appropriate or it may be a teacher with specific skills, training or interest in that area. The most obvious co-ordinator is the one responsible for art in the school. They might have some ideas for displaying mathematics that you had not considered; also working with science and humanities co-ordinators to look at the ways statistical information is displayed and how this might enhance the profile of the mathematical skills used within their subjects. Talking to the English co-ordinator about book displays of mathematics, either commercially produced or produced in school may give you both ideas for display and the acquisition of books for the library to support the teaching and learning of mathematics.

> ### Task
>
> Look around your setting/school to see if the mathematics on display focuses on mathematics as a separate subject or is there work that emphases the cross-curricular nature of the skills and knowledge? Can you name a mathematician? If not what do you think that says about the image of mathematics as a subject?

Promoting the image of mathematics as not just a western subject is also important in a changing setting/school population. You might involve parents who are artistic and who could assist with displays. You might also be able to use the parent's knowledge of games and number systems from other countries to display in school. Displays might include counting in other languages/scripts with tapes of audio so that children can listen to how the language sounds when someone uses them to count. Collections of calculating devices from around the world can be starting points for explorations and discussions about how they work, for example a Soroban.

Task

Can you name any women mathematicians? If not why do you think this is the case?

You may have thought of Ada Lovelace (1815–52) who was the daughter of Lord Bryon and credited for her work with Charles Babbage in establishing the field of what was to become computer science. Another English woman mathematician was Mary Somerville (1780–1872) after whom Somerville College in Oxford is named; she worked in the area of algebra.

Mathematics is often considered a 'male' subject and so it is important that there are role models for girls. One way is to display information about women and mathematics including women mathematicians; who they were/are and their contribution to mathematics. Displaying information about mathematicians can start a discussion of what a mathematician might do as their work, specifically with KS2.

Task

Find out about mathematicians and display information about them either in the classroom or the setting/school. Or a group of children can find out about a mathematician; can they present the information for others? Could they also present the information using PowerPoint to the rest of the class/school?

Display outdoors

Raising awareness of mathematics doesn't always have to focus on indoor activity. The playground or field can be the site for mathematical activity. Firstly look at what is there already, are there faded number lines of hopscotch games. What would be suitable resources to explore within the schools grounds that will be durable and not attract vandals? The following are some suggestions of things you might want to think about with ideas of how they might be used to teach and learn mathematics. Any of these can be painted onto playground surfaces like ground and/or walls.

> **Task**
>
> What resources are there outside that you could use for display? How might you link this to the trails described in Chapter 10?

Number squares

Range might include
100 number square, or one that goes past 100 to show how to write larger numbers, one including negative numbers, a blank number square, a blank number line, number lines in different languages.

Use
Games, looking for multiples, physically moving up and down number lines, marking the difference between objects or people on the number line.

Games

Range might include
Hopscotch, snakes and ladders, chess board.

Use
Counting, rules of games.

Patterns and others

Range might include
Repeating patterns of shapes.

Use
People mathematics.

Be aware of the issue of images that are created for children by displays in and outside the building. A display of painted shapes on a wall is fine but when numbers are added to the centre of the shapes it changes the image and the connections made by the children. Is a 5 inside a rectangle helpful for the children to make associations between number and shape for example?

Task

Task

There is a tendency to consider outdoors and outdoor display as being most appropriate for the Early Years. KS2 children can benefit from stimuli outside the classroom. This can be as simple as a question or as complicated as a chessboard with pieces in the environment.

This chapter is designed to provoke an examination of the use of display in the creative teaching of mathematics. It is not intended to provide all the answers but to start the process of thinking creatively about the mathematical environment offered to children.

CHAPTER 10

Field trips for mathematics

This chapter will focus on the idea of planning a specific trip focusing on mathematics, which may be a new idea to many. Most school trips are focused around the humanities and so this chapter seeks to change the view of trips so they can support mathematics teaching and learning and provide a creative stimulus for this process.

Where can you find mathematics?

Mathematicians would say that mathematics is all around us and so any trip would contain mathematical elements.

Planning a trip

If children are involved in planning activities they can focus on the costs, number of coaches and adults needed as part of the process; this can be a source of mathematical activity. The more the problems and the ideas come from the children the more it becomes 'real problem solving' rather than adult-led problems. If children are involved in planning they need to know the constraints, such as cost and distance, before they start getting carried away with trips to theme parks in other countries. Although the adults have the responsibilities for the risk assessments and the control of the trips children can be involved. Table 10.1 begins to explore the advantages and disadvantages of the children's involvement. This list, which you may want to read and reflect upon is not exhaustive.

> *Task*
>
> When you are next planning a trip consider how the children could become more involved. You may find it helpful to write down your own version of the advantages and disadvantages to look at the barriers that may be affecting children's involvement. What are your concerns? Are your concerns based upon experience? How could things be completed differently that would change your concerns?

Table 10.1 Advantages and disadvantages of children's involvement in trip planning

Advantages of children's involvement in planning trips	Disadvantages of children's involvement in planning trips
The children feel more ownership of the ideas and plans.	The adults may feel less in control of the focus of the trip.
The children have the opportunity to think about budgets and how to work within one.	Adults may feel less in control of the mathematics that is being used and/or learnt during the planning process.
Children learn how to communicate to all parties involved, orally and where necessary in writing.	Adults may not be comfortable with children communicating with the other parties involved.
Children learn how to plan and consider time lines within their plans.	There may be adult frustrations because of the time factors involved in the planning and organising processes.
Children learn to co-operate and to take responsibility for different parts of the task.	There may be adult frustrations because of lack of co-operation. Adults may feel they will spend all their time sorting out squabbles.
Children have the opportunity to extend their knowledge and learn new skills. They may need to gain new skills in order to complete the process.	Children may need to gain new skills in order to complete the process. This may lead to frustrations.
Children learn to reflect upon the processes (this can be linked to the journaling ideas in Chapter 7)	Adults may feel there is limited mathematics to reflect on at the end of the process.

The journey as a source of mathematical opportunities

Coach journeys would allow for planning the route before the journey to work out which route would be the shortest, longest, avoids motorway travel, and allows for stops if necessary. Estimating how much fuel would be used and the time for the journeys would also be possible for KS2 children. This links knowledge from map reading in geography.

For younger children the journey could be used for looking out for signs and symbols whilst they travel, as suggested below (see Figure 10.1). You can decide on the number of each item the children have got to spot during the journey, for example yellow cars. Teams of children can be tasked to look out for different kinds of vehicles, keeping a score to see which company has more vehicles on the route, e.g. Eddie Stobart, Leggetts, and Norbert Dentressangle. The winning team will have spotted the most of their vehicles. It is worth having someone to keep all the scores to act as an umpire in case of disputed sightings of lorry types. Another idea is for

Figure 10.1 Things to find on our journey

children to write down unusual number plates including the places of origin and when back in the class finding out which vehicle has come from the furthest to this country. The children could also make their own grids either for themselves or for each other as part of the planning for the journey. Journeys can be difficult parts of the trip with a number of children and so activities can prevent the inevitable cries of 'Are we there yet?' or similar and help with keeping the children occupied en route. An alternative is that children can be given a clipboard and pencil on the coach or other transport and asked to write down questions about the journey, with the answers, that they can ask others when they are back in the classroom. There is a health and safety warning required for considering this kind of task and that is children can become travel sick because they are reading or writing. An alternative for individuals who find travelling difficult is essential.

Where to go to explore mathematics?

For young children a group trip to the local shop to buy provisions for a cooking activity could be a simple answer to exploring the mathematics. Here the children can explore the number of items required and some aspects of the costs of things bought. The following section of this chapter looks at some places that are commonly used for school/Early Years setting trips, often as the focus of other areas of learning/curriculum. The intention is to get the reader to look at these locations with 'mathematical eyes' and to see the potential in exploring mathematics in these locations. As in other chapters it is not intended to provide an exhaustive list of potential locations for trips but to show what is possible within a range of trips.

Supermarkets and other shops

One popular visit that children are likely to undertake during the Early Years and/or Primary age range is a trip to the local shops. Often the main focus of this visit is healthy eating and/or buying items for cooking. These are good sources of information that can be used with different age groups to explore mathematics. Table 10.2 shows just a few ideas with the different age groups from a visit to the shops.

Art galleries

The connections between art and mathematics may not appear obvious but art can be a very stimulating starting point for mathematics. At a simple level, calculating

Table 10.2 Shops across the age range

	Foundation stage	KS1	KS2
Tinned food	Identifying the shape of tins and what is stored in them. How can tins be stacked?	Comparison of prices of tinned items. Number of tins in boxes.	Brand comparison by price, average contents by weight or by volume.
Fresh foods	Numbers of types of specific foods. Sorting fruit and vegetables as an example.	Patterns of packaging including multiples of items. Sell-by and use-by dates – how long does fresh food last?	Distance travelled by food from different countries, distances in miles and kilometres. Differences in wholesale and retail costs.
Bread	Shapes and sizes. Cost of loaves of bread. Number of slices in loaves.	Sandwiches, halves and quarters, triangles and squares.	Costs, weights, ingredients, amount of wrapping paper needed to wrap a loaf.

how long ago a painting or other work of art was completed provides a connection and a use for mathematics. The length of time an artist lived and how old he/she was when they completed a specific piece is again a reason for calculations.

The National Gallery in London provides web-based information about a range of pictures in the gallery and zoomable images that can be downloaded to an IWB for a virtual gallery tour without leaving the school or setting (www.nationalgallery.org.uk/education/teachers_notes/default.htm).

The gallery makes suggestions of connections for the chosen pictures, for example *The Hay Wain* by John Constable. Mathematical activities based on sorting plants, animals, man-made things, things which make a noise, things that can move. Or *The Stonemason's Yard* by Canaletto with a focus on shapes, 2-D and 3-D and/or plotting co-ordinates by making a grid over the picture and asking children to locate objects within the picture. This last suggestion could be completed with any picture with lots of details.

The National Gallery also has a programme of activities around taking one picture each year to explore with teachers in detail for work with their class. Details of this programme can be found on www.takeonepicture.org.

The choice of the picture that you might use as the basis of work, not just in mathematics, will depend upon the learning objectives which you plan to cover during the period of study. Choosing a picture painted at a specific time of the year can generate discussion about seasons and the passage of time which is a difficult concept for many children to grasp in the Early Years and Primary ages. Older children could be challenged to find out the proportion of one colour used in a picture like

Composition with Red, Yellow and Blue (1921) by Piet Mondrian. This artist is famous for the use of straight lines and coloured regions within his work which could be another area of exploration.

The Tate also has a number of resources available for teachers on www.tate.org.uk This could enable you to focus on any or all of the following works of art (see Table 10.3).

Table 10.3 Art and mathematics

Work of art	Mathematical focus
painting entitled *Laci and Lucia* by László Moholy-Nagy	reflections and symmetry
painting entitled *Landscape of Shame* by Cedric Morris	shape and space
picture entitled *Sandblasted Glass with Black Paint* by Josef Albers	shape and space, number of squares, proportions of different colours, proportion, fraction, ratio of black in the picture
picture entitled *Structural Constellations* by Josef Albers	shape and space, lines and regions
sculpture entitled *Man Taking off his Shirt* by Anthony Caro	shape and space
sculptures by Antony Gormley	space and scale

Task

Can you plan and use either a trip to an art gallery or a virtual tour to explore a starting point for the children to investigate?

Museums

Different kinds of museums allow for a variety of approaches to mathematics. For example, the Northampton Museum and Art Gallery has a large collection of shoes and boots as this area is famous for the manufacture of footwear. The oldest shoe in this collection is an Egyptian sandal sole, 2200 BC, and so this provides for work on the passage of time, differences in time and ages of exhibits in the museum. There are several footwear size scales. Another interesting issue is how we get shoe sizes. The most common in Britain has sizes that are one third of an inch long which is the length of three barleycorns and it is said it was decreed by Edward II as such in 1324, but there is no proof of this. Again, there are a number of investigations that can be completed in relation to measuring feet in the class, comparing the sizes of shoes and the measures used at different periods in history. The cost of a pair of shoes at different points in history provides interesting data to compare, for example a pair of riding boots cost 9d in 1266. How much would a similar pair of boots cost today and how do the costs compare in real terms?

Other parts of the country also have museums dedicated to footwear such as The Shoe Museum in Street in Somerset. Alternatively, some large museums have collections that include footwear which could be the focus of a trip, such as the Victoria and Albert Museum in London or the Milton Keynes Museum which has a collection of running shoes. The latter could be part of a sports topic which could include distances of various races, the measurements used to set out the track, the speed of the runners, differences in world records, as just a few examples. This might be combined with a trip to a sporting venue or specific sporting museum like the Rugby Museum.

Table 10.4 guides some other suggestions for other trips to museums.

A full alphabetical list of museums in the UK is available on vlmp. museophile.com/uk.html.

Task

Can you plan and use either a trip to a museum or a virtual tour to explore a starting point for the children to investigate?

Trips using the natural world

Trips to a wooded area can be a good source of data to use in mathematics, from counting the number of specific plants and trees to calculating the height of a tree. This is a place where non-standard measures can be used for discovering how many people it takes to reach around a tree trunk, as an example.

Mathematics trails

These can be created in the setting or school grounds or in other spaces outside the institution. These are the mathematical version of a nature trail and they are designed to:

- encourage children to find mathematics in their environment
- introduce children to the wonder of mathematics
- help children to observe things from a different perspective

- encourage children to see how mathematics is used in the environment in which we live
- help children to appreciate the interrelationship between mathematics and the environment
- help children see the relevance of mathematics outside the classroom
- help children to appreciate the aesthetic beauty in mathematics.

Table 10.4 Museums and mathematics

Museums	Mathematical focus
Royal Armouries – Leeds	Shapes of shields, coats of arms for men and women – roundel/lozegene, lengths of spears, comparison of length of spears with soldiers' heights, working out heights of people from their armour.
Fleet Air Arm Museum – Yeovilton	Lots of opportunities for measuring and looking at measuring instruments at a museum like this. Age of aircraft. Number of crew in any one aircraft. Speeds of aircraft.
Postal Museum – Bath	Weights and measures, postage stamps and their cost, sizes of letters, links to *Postman Pat* stories. Ages of old letters. Loan boxes available to schools and settings local to the museum. Sizes and shapes and colours of postboxes. Sizes of letter boxes. Numbers in addresses and post codes.
Cadbury World – Birmingham	Weights and measures, number of squares in a bar of chocolate, amounts of specific ingredients in making chocolate, shapes and sizes, using cocoa beans as money, links with Aztecs and the Aztec calendar which leads into telling the time, patterns and designs, how much paper is used to cover a bar of chocolate with foil, with the paper sleeve or other covering. Rates of production of the bars of chocolate by specific machines.
British Museum, London	This museum has a wide variety of collections from the UK and worldwide. Ancient Greek coinage, currencies from Africa including cowrie shells. Looking at compasses to show direction.
National Coal Mining Museum	Loan boxes are available from this museum – details on the website. Opportunities for measurements of mines, depth of shafts, wages paid to miners at different points in history, amounts an individual miner would have dug in a shift, shift hours expected underground.

In working along a mathematics trail children are encouraged to:

- follow instructions
- record information in words, numbers and symbols
- collect information
- estimate measurements
- count objects
- observe and gather a range of examples of tessellations and symmetry
- use numbers to solve problems and questions on the trail.

There may be other skills and knowledge used depending upon the kinds of questions asked.

Why create a mathematics trail?

- to familiarise children either with a new context, new school or location that they are visiting
- to offer an opportunity to use and apply mathematics already learnt
- to provide a variety of different contexts in which mathematical ideas can occur
- to encourage children to work together
- to emphasise the cross-curricular links
- as a project for older children making a trail for younger learners making use of their mathematical skills and knowledge
- to offer a purpose for recording information mathematically
- to offer a different perspective on mathematics
- to foster children's awareness of the world around them
- to add enjoyment.

Writing and setting up a mathematics trail requires a fair amount of work but can be an opportunity for teachers to work together to plan a trail either for a year group or the setting or school. If your setting/school has interesting grounds then this is the safest and easiest place to plan your trail. The next issue to consider is the age of the children as this will alter the kind of trail you will devise. For young children, markers can be placed at key points to keep them on the trail whereas older children may not require this additional support. If questions are placed on the trail then different age groups or abilities can be directed to different-coloured clues. If you want children to record as they go along the trail then you also need to plan for clipboards and pencils in order that they can record easily.

The most successful mathematics trails include questions that can be answered at the time, for instance how many steps can you see from the path to the pond? They also include activities that can be extended at a later date in the classroom and/or at home, for example collect three different-shaped leaves. This can lead to comparison in the classroom and also a home task to find more whilst out playing. Trails may also include collecting information which can be collated later using a database or spreadsheet, e.g. number of cars parked in a specific location. Other activities may involve recognition of numbers and shapes either with a picture clue or specific place to stand to carry out the recognition task. Examples might include presenting a jumbled-up picture of a street or set of buildings and asking the children to put them in the right order. Or which shapes can you see in the building in front of you when you stand on the X?

Writing the trail

Consider carefully the length of the trail so that it is long enough for an in-depth activity but not too long that the children and the adult will get bored and restless. For young children the trail doesn't need to be written but can be hidden shapes and numbers along a given route which the children have to draw in a coloured grid. If there are questions for the young children then an adult needs to be planned into the activity to support them. This can be an opportunity for assessing children in a small group and for encouraging mathematical talk. You also need to work out the answers you are expecting from the activities as these can form part of the discussion afterwards. With digital photographs and an IWB this can be a colourful activity in the classroom. Children could be asked to take a camera with them on the trail, taking pictures as part of their recording. These would also make a good display emphasising the cross-curricular nature of mathematics.

When constructing your trail organise it so that there are clearly defined stopping points at which questions can be answered. Consider the height of the line of sight of the children, so you may need to crouch down to see what they see or can't see when devising the questions. Allow time for discussion at the stopping points – a crucial part of the briefing for any adults working with small groups. Allow time for children to find things on crowded and busy notice boards and to find the key pieces of information needed.

Extracts from mathematics trails

These are to give you an idea of some of the kinds of questions you might use in your own trail and they depend upon the environment you are going to use for your trail.

Early Years

1. What is next to the door?
2. What shape are the bricks in the wall?
3. Can you make a wall of brick in the builders' tray outside?
4. Can you make a rubbing of a brick?
5. Can you go through a square shape on the climbing frame?
6. Count the windows on this side of the classroom.
7. Find the number 4 on the snakes on the playground.
8. Find the red square on the tree. Turn so this is behind you. What can you see?
9. Find a round drain cover and make a rubbing of the pattern.
10. How many steps can you take along the willow tunnel?
11. Find a yellow duck in the sandpit. What number does it have on it?
12. Find an interesting shape to bring back into the classroom with you.

For KS1

1. Record what the time is now on your clock face.
2. How many steps into the playground?
3. Find an air brick. Close your eyes, estimate and then record the number of holes there are in it. Draw the air brick.
4. Can you add up the numbers on the snake on the playground? Record your answer.
5. Look at the Y1 classroom. Close your eyes. Estimate how many panes of glass there are in the windows. Count and record.
6. Find and draw three cylinders in the playground.
7. Can you find the drain cover? Draw the part of the cover which you think is interesting. Is this a symmetrical pattern?
8. Can you find any triangles? Record where you found them.
9. Which bikes are in the parking bays in the Foundation stage area?
10. Record what the time is now.
11. How long did it take you to complete the trail.
12. Draw a plan of your route.

For KS2

1. Start your stopwatch now. This will allow you to time yourself on the trail.
2. How many large litter bins are there in the playground?

How many small litter bins are there in the playground?

Are there fewer of the large or small bins? Why do you think this is the case?

3. What is the circumference of the top of one of the large bins?

4. Add all the numbers of the hopscotch. What is this number a multiple of?

5. How many cars are parked in the car park? Make a note of the time of day.

6. How many books in the library? How could you estimate the number?

7. Where could you be standing on rectangles, looking through squares at triangles?

8. Find something, which has an octagon, two circles and lots of diamonds.

9. Find the spiral numbers in blue and yellow. Could you total _ by walking in a straight line across the whole or part of the spiral?

10. Stop the stop watch now that you have finished the trail.

11. How long did the trail take you? Give your answer in seconds.

Task

Using the examples and guidance given in this chapter can you plan a mathematics trail in or outside your setting/school? This is a good opportunity to work with colleagues and share different perspectives on the same environment so that this becomes a learning opportunity for you professionally as well as the development of a shared resource. Maybe the whole staff group could get involved in the process of writing and trialling the trail.

In this chapter the field trips for mathematics can be as short a distance as the setting or school grounds or it can be a trip, which is further afield. Although this kind of activity requires a substantial amount of planning and preparation on the part of the adults, the benefits are enormous in terms of the enjoyment and mathematical learning that is possible. They are well worth a go.

CHAPTER 11

The sky's the limit

This chapter explores where you might go next and will look briefly at some of the current innovatives that could be used to support the development of creative teaching and learning of mathematics across the Early Years and Primary age range. The chapter will also look at issues for moving forward with developing creativity in mathematics.

Creative Partnerships

The innovative of Creative Partnerships was set up in 2002 to give young people in disadvantaged areas across England the opportunity to develop their creativity and ambition by forming partnerships between schools and creative organisations, businesses and individuals. In their evaluation of the innovative, Ofsted found that schools participating in the innovative stimulated pupils' creativity and established the conditions in which pupils can further develop their creative skills. Children benefited from working alongside creative practitioners such as writers, designers, entrepreneurs, artists and performers which enhanced motivation and encouraged high aspirations. It was not just the children and young people's creative skills that developed but for many there were significant improvements in literacy, numeracy and Information and Communication Technology. The intention behind the Creative Partnerships is to build relationships between schools, creative individuals and appropriate organisations for the purpose of changing:

- the approach and attitudes of teachers
- the practice of creative individuals and organisations
- the aspiration and performance of young people.

The Creative Partnerships involve large numbers of schools and organisations, training adults from the creative sector to work in schools. For this project, they chose the following definition of creativity:

'Creativity is defined in this survey as a combination of meanings expressed by the National Advisory Committee on Creative and Cultural Education. (NACCCE): imaginative activity fashioned so as to produce outcomes that are both original and of value and the National Endowment for Science, Technology and the Arts (NESTA): seeing what no one else has seen, thinking what no one else has thought and doing what no one else has dared.'

Some of the creative partners in the project are scientists, geographers and historians. There is still the danger that Creative Partnerships are perceived as mainly serving curriculum development and enrichment in the arts rather than as a resource for the whole school. Eames, Benton, Sharp, and Kendall (2006) looked at the impact on young people within the project achievements. They found that when compared with similar young people nationally, young people who attended Creative Partnerships activities made either similar or slightly better progress in their National Curriculum assessments. Those known to have attended Creative Partnerships activities out-performed those in the same schools but not known to have attended Creative Partnerships activities, by a small but statistically significant extent at all three key stages.

Task

You may have a Creative Partnership in place in your setting or school. These are usually artists in residence in the Early Years and Primary school. Could you consider someone with a mathematical or scientific role who might come and work within your setting or school? This may not be for a lengthy stay but could show children the more creative side of these roles.

Linked to the Creative Partnerships' evaluation of the role of the creative individuals working in schools is the work highlighting the role of the teacher in providing a guided support for the development of children's creativity. Tegano, Moran and Sawyer (1991), for example, suggest that teachers and other adults can encourage creativity by behaviours such as:

- asking open-ended questions
- tolerating ambiguity
- modelling creative thinking and behaviour
- encouraging experimentation and persistence
- praising children who provide unexpected answers.

> **Task**
>
> How might you work as a team to develop the approaches suggested above to guide and support the development of children's creativity?

Breaking free of the mathematical stereotype

Mathematics as a subject has a stereotypical image, which is discussed in Chapter 1. How might we develop the teaching and learning of mathematics to break free from this stereotype? Instead of thinking about specific aspects of mathematics or for specific groups, we could focus on what makes good mathematics education. This should incorporate an approach that is an enriching and stimulating experience for all children and, some would argue, the teacher, in order to stimulate their development in teaching and continue their interest in learning. ENRICH suggest that this approach should include content opportunities designed to:

- develop and use problem-solving strategies
- encourage mathematical thinking
- include historical cultural contexts
- offer opportunities for mathematical extension.

Therefore, this enrichment is not simply learning facts and demonstrating skills. Mathematical skills and knowledge can be precursors to, and outcomes of, an enrichment curriculum.

The aim of an enrichment curriculum is to support:

- a problem-solving approach
- improving pupil attitudes
- a growing appreciation of mathematics
- the development of conceptual structures.

(Adapted from Ernest 2000)

In the earlier chapters of this book this approach has been the central focus of the ideas, suggestions and questions raised about the creative learning and teaching of mathematics. This suggests a different focus for mathematics educators as Tobias (undated) suggests we should be modelling, stimulating and rewarding creativity and above all not punishing creativity.

Lessons from overseas

What can we learnt about creative mathematics from looking overseas? How have other countries engaged with the notions of creativity in education and specifically in mathematics? One common problem that there is in the materials from other countries is the combination of creativity and the gifted child. In the USA the focus is clearly on gifted and talented, as can be seen in this extract from Miller (1990): 'Although mathematically talented students display creativity when dealing with mathematical ideas, this is not always apparent in creativity test results. However, high creativity assessments, along with indications of intense interest in mathematics, do seem to be a significant clue of mathematical talent.' Tobias (undated) sees fostering creativity in mathematics as a way of overcoming mathematics anxiety, increasing the learners' successes with mathematics as she argues that it is not enough to generate creative technical people. Others educators in the USA combine creativity only with open-ended problems and on the engagement of older learners with the same aim as the Creative Partnerships in England. Creative mathematics searches in relation to the USA reveal plenty of materials for worksheets linked to topics and 'math centers' as they are described. The latter appear to be areas created in the classroom for children to choose to work in, which are reminiscent of earlier work on areas or bays for specific subject areas in the UK.

In Germany, Meissner (2000) describes a project entitled 'We build a village' which concentrated on geometry to further geometry concepts of both plane and three-dimensional geometry in Primary schools. In this module for Primary grades (age about 8–10 years) the children worked with about 35 different solids, made of styrofoam, wood, paper nets, or plastic. The activities for the children were diverse and consisted of sorting and classifying, folding, drawing, cutting, constructing nets, using plasticine, and building solids and houses with these models. At the end of the module (of about seven lessons) the children build their own village with a grocery store, a church, a school, and other houses, as well as a creek, streets and parking areas. This kind of topic approach to teaching and learning is moving back into the Primary curriculum with the introduction of the ideas from the Primary Strategy (DfES 2003) and the subsequent continuing professional development materials. This is enabling teachers to look again at the ways they are constructing the learning to engage children with mathematics and to learn to become creative mathematicians.

Marie-Thérèse Loeman (2002) from Belgium has written about a European project 'How to learn from and make history in mathematics'. Although this is with Secondary school children, the work mirrors some of the ideas explored in Chapters 3 and 7 in this book.

Takahashi (2006) describes the characteristics of Japanese mathematics lessons for the Primary age range as including a significant amount of problem solving. This teaching approach is called 'structured problem solving' and is designed to create interest in mathematics and stimulate creative mathematical activity in the classroom. A big part of the teaching style is the emphasis on children's collaborative work. Lessons usually start with children working individually to solve a problem using their own mathematical knowledge. After working on the problems, children bring various approaches and solutions to classroom discussion. We would recognise this as a mini plenary or interim review. The teacher then leads children in a whole-class discussion in order to compare individual approaches and solutions. The Japanese suggest that this whole-class activity provides children with opportunities to develop their mathematical abilities including conceptual and procedural understanding. An interesting issue for the UK is that the Japanese teacher, although leading the discussion, is not directly teaching but facilitating the children's learning at least in these structured problem-solving lessons. The aim of this approach is to develop students' understanding of mathematical concepts and skills and the teacher is expected to facilitate mathematical discussion for children to achieve this aim. This discussion is often called neriage' in Japanese, which implies 'polishing ideas' (Takahashi 2006). This could be seen as in marked contrast to the direct teaching emphasised with the introduction of the NNS. Japanese teachers use the blackboard to show diagrams, graphs, drawings and to record ideas. Yoshida (2005) describes how Japanese teachers use the blackboard or 'bansho':

- to keep a record of the lesson
- to help children remember what they need to do and to think about
- to help children see the connection between different parts of the lesson and the progression of the lesson
- to compare, contrast, and discuss ideas that children present
- to help to organise children's thinking and discovery of new ideas
- to foster organised children's note-taking skills by modelling good organisation.

(Adapted from Yoshida 2005)

Although we have largely moved from blackboards to whiteboards and IWBs, the principles of supporting a child-centred approach to learning mathematics could be used in UK classrooms.

What have we learnt from looking at other countries? There is the same range of responses to defining creativity in mathematics in other countries. Creativity is mainly associated with a narrow view of mathematics as problem solving. There is also a tendency to concentrate on only more able children who are seen as being creative. The role of the teacher or adult working with children is important as from

Japan comes the lesson of facilitating rather than giving a specific rubric for problem solving. Discussion is important for all children to be involved in working on ideas and potential solutions and the board work by the teacher keeps a clear record for children to refer back to through the process.

In Finland, number one in the PISA (2003) studies for numeracy and literacy the approach to all education is decentralised with flexibility to local needs including at individual school level. 'There is no centralised system for approval for textbooks – variety in this respect is seen as a necessary component for functional autonomy in methods of teaching.' (Bjorkqvist 2005) The teaching is in small mixed-ability groups, again with lots of discussion as the basis of the teaching approach. Finland was considered first in mathematical literacy and problem solving for the 15-year-olds tested. There is clearly a good grounding in earlier mathematical learning.

Task

Consider the approaches and ideas from other countries. Which do you think are most thought provoking? Which ideas will you try out in your own teaching?

Use of technology

A BECTA project of 2002, 'ICT used to promote pupils creativity across the curriculum', suggested that using ICT allowed children to pursue initial questions but also to allow these to be replaced by a new direction if that occurred. The environment created by the use of ICT encouraged children to take risks with possible solutions and there was no punishment for wrong answers. The medium of ICT allowed for sharing of ideas with others. For the Early Years and Primary age group a project like 'Playground' may hold some answers where children between the ages of 4 and 8 play, design and create games within a computer environment. The aim of the project is to harness children's playfulness, creative potential and exploratory spirit, allowing them to enter into formal and abstract ways of thinking. Playground was a three-year EU-funded project (1998–2001), with academic and commercial partners in the UK, Portugal, Slovakia and Sweden. The environments created allowed children to work on problems, making them their own and redesigning problems within the environments.

Although designed for higher mathematics, a program like 'Visumath' allows children to see shapes created in terms of function of the surfaces of 3-D objects and 2-D graphs, as this shows some of the beauty of mathematics. This kind of project will support the development of children's visualisation skills.

Technology is also part of the 'Be Very Afraid' showcase of innovations introduced in Chapter 5. The opportunities created with mobile technology allow children to explore their environment whilst recording notes on hand-held devices to bring back into the classroom space and download to a display for the whole class to see.

Mathematics education has perhaps been afraid of technology with an emphasis on calculations mentally or in written form. Reaching for a calculator has implied a lack of ability. Yet calculators have a place in releasing children from the routine procedures to focus on other specific areas of development. Examples include the use of graphical calculators (Gray and Pitta 1997) to stimulate the construction of mental imagery associated directly with arithmetical symbols as opposed to imagery that is an analogical transformation to them. The imagery of 'higher achievers' tended to be symbolic and was used by the children to support the production of known and derived facts. The 'lower achievers' tended to be analogical representations of physical objects. 'Emily' is described as a 'low achiever' working with a graphical calculator in order to change her imagery. The results from this research work suggested that Emily was building a different range of meanings associated with numbers and numerical symbolism as a result of the program developed for use with the calculator. She was moving away from a reliance on counting procedures. This research shows a creative use of calculators to effect changes in an individual's mental imagery and therefore her success with arithmetic.

Pratt (1995) described the graphing work of eight-and nine-year-olds who have immediate and continuous access to portable computers across the curriculum. The children used the computers to generate graphs and charts from experimental data. Pratt draws out two distinct uses of the graphing facilities available in spreadsheet software. The first is passive graphing which is where children use a graph to display the results of an experiment and consequently the children come to see the graph as a presentational tool. The information is collated at the end of the process and therefore the children using this approach made only pseudo-mathematical connections between the graph and the data. The second is active graphing which is where the children use the graph to help them decide on the next action to be taken in the experiment. They are encouraged to generate the graph after the collection of only a few pieces of data; as they continue to collect the data more graphs are drawn and interpretations made. The children are using the graphing as a meaningful and relevant tool. 'The child who sees graphing as an analytical instrument has made a powerful mathematical connection which has fundamentally widened that child's grasp of the utility of graphing.' (Pratt 1995: 165)

Task

Consider what technology is available to you in order to develop your teaching creatively for mathematics. What difference does technology make to the possibilities available for teaching and learning?

Issues for moving forward with developing creativity in mathematics

What stops us developing creative approaches to the teaching and learning in a specific area of the curriculum? Is it just the time to do things differently? Is it lack of confidence? The fear of accountability? Lack of resources? The following is a potential action plan depending upon the barriers to developments.

Accountability

Although this is important, the guidance from the PNS and the agendas of personalised learning and ECM are all focusing on reducing the barriers to learning for all children. A creative approach to teaching and learning mathematics can reduce the barriers for children and offer them a different view of mathematics as a subject.

Confidence

To increase your confidence of working in a different way don't try to change everything at once. Try to introduce one different way of working from one of the chapters in this book and build on your confidence of working in this way. Remember the strengths you have in teaching other areas of the curriculum, these are confidences you can draw on. What could you transfer to the teaching of mathematics?

Controlling the learning

Teachers often worry about their own subject knowledge in mathematics. Although subject knowledge is important for making the connections between aspects of mathematics, it is not necessary to know everything that children might encounter in working in more open-ended ways. Developing the confidence to learn alongside the children is important, finding sources that are useful to support all learners with the activites. It is important to check definitions or other information before committing to answer children's queries as misinformation can result in misconceptions in the future. Keeping careful mapping of the mathematics areas covered and achieved in any open-ended task is crucial for future planning and is a source of information when needed for accountability.

Planning for a creative approach

Planning the time allocated for children to work on open-ended tasks is important. They will need more space than a single mathematics lesson or a clear link between work started in session/lessons on different days. Again, start small and build up to longer more cross-curricular sessions. Start with an area of your own interest, for example books, films, scientific problem solving as this will help your confidence and stimulate your own interests further.

Time

Time has two issues. The first is your time to plan new activities. This doesn't have to be a difficulty as there are lots of resources for starting points in this book, in your setting/school and on the internet. The other issue of time is the space for the children and you to learn together as outlined earlier. In the long run the time to plan for this approach is no longer than normal planning and it is also likely to be a more pleasurable experience for you as this is more fun.

Resources

Most people think about teaching and learning resources as needing to be expensive but in the chapters throughout this book there are simple resources which can be easily collected by adults and children. Resources like IWBs and mobile technology are becoming more commonplace in classrooms. You might challenge yourself to develop the use of one new ICT resource each term and you will be well on your way to developing your expertise. Resources can also mean the people involved and it is crucial to discuss any new approaches with your teaching team so everyone is clear about the expectations of interventions and of tasks. There are colleagues who are resources of ideas and expertise which you can draw upon. You might find that undertaking some team teaching with a colleague who has more confidence and/or experience of more open-ended activities would support your own developments in mathematics.

Involving children

Children are a key source of inspiration for adults working with them. Their innocent questions or sudden interests can be the starting point for investigative and creative mathematics. The child who wants to know about dinosaurs or brings something in to show can spark scaling dinosaur footprints or counting the petals on flowers. Real-life problem solving is only really worth pursuing if the starting point comes from the children. Can we mark out a proper football pitch so those who don't want to play football have a clear space to play at playtime? This would then involve the children in marking out a clear boundary and considering how to keep footballs from straying outside the given space.

> ### Task
> Pick a starting point for yourself that links to some of the potential actions outlined. Make a note of how you will develop your creative teaching of mathematics.

Where next?

The whole of this book, we hope, will act as a resource for developing a creative approach to the teaching and learning of mathematics across the Early Years and Primary age range. Reading this may have made you more aware of the images of mathematics as a subject and the kinds of creativity possible within the domain. We hope this book will alert you to the possible examples of children's creativity within mathematics. Being a creative teacher of mathematics is possible for everyone if starting small and building upon existing strengths in teaching approaches potentially drawn from expertise demonstrated in other subjects. Remember the sky's the limit!

References

Alcuin (c. 800) *Propositiones alcuini doctoris caroli magni imperatoris ad acuendos juvenes* (Problems for the Quickening of the Minds of the Young). Available: en.wikipedia.org/wiki/Alcuin.

Askew, M., Brown, M., Rhodes, V., Wiliam, D. and Johnson, D. (1997) *Effective Teachers of Numeracy: A Report of a Study Carried out for the Teacher Training Agency*. London: King's College, University of London.

Austin, P. (1998) 'Math books as literature: which ones measure up?', *New Advocate*, 11(2): 119–133.

Avital, S. (1995) 'History of mathematics can help improve instruction and learning', in Swetz, F.J., Fauvel, J., Bekken, O., Johansson, B. and Katz, V. (eds) *Learn from the Masters!* Washington, DC: Mathematical Association of America, pp. 3–12.

Barker, J. (2006) *Agincourt*. London: Abacus.

Bidwell, J. (1993) 'Humanize Your Classroom with the History of Mathematics', *Mathematics Teacher*, 86: 461–464.

Bjorkqvist, O. (2005) *Mathematics education in Finland – what makes it work?* Available: www.math.unipa.it/~grim/21_project/21_malasya_Bjorkqvist45–48_05.pdf.

Briggs, M. (1998) 'The right baggage?', in Olivier, A. and Newstead, K. (1998) (eds) *Proceedings of the 22nd Conference of the International Group for the Psychology of Mathematics Education*. South Africa: Stellenbosch, pp. 152–159.

Briggs, M. (2000) 'Feel free to be flexible', *Special Children*, 125: 1–8.

Briggs, M. (2001) 'Planning', in Mooney, C., Briggs, M., Fletcher, M. and McCullouch, J. (eds) *Primary Mathematics: Teaching Theory and Practice*. Exeter: Learning Matters, pp. 118–144.

Briggs, M., Daniell, J., Farncombe, J., Lenton, N. and Stonehouse, A. (2002) 'Wizarding maths'. *Mathematics Teaching*, 180: 23–27.

Briggs, M. (2005) 'Creative mathematics', in Wilson, A. (ed.) *Creativity in Primary Education: Theory and Practice*. Exeter: Learning Matters, pp. 102–111.

Bruce, T. (2004) *Cultivating Creativity in Babies, Toddlers and Young Children*. London: Hodder Arnold.

Burton, L. (1990) 'What could teacher education be like for prospective teachers of early childhood mathematics? – with particular reference to the environment', in Steffe, L. and Woods, T. (eds) *Transforming Children's Mathematics Education: International Perspectives*. Hillsdale, NJ: Lawrence Erlbaum.

Buxton, L. (1981) *Do you Panic about Mathematics?* London: Heinemann.

Coles, D. and Copeland, T. (2002) *Numeracy and Mathematics across the Primary Curriculum: Building Confidence and Understanding*. London: David Fulton.

Craft, A. (2002) *Creativity and Early Years Education: A Lifewide Foundation*. London: Continuum.

Craft, A. (2003) 'The limits to creativity in education: dilemmas for the educator', *British Journal of Educational Studies*, 51(2): 113–127.

Cropley, A.J. (2001) *Creativity in Education and Learning: A Guide for Teachers and Educators*. London and Sterling: Kogan Page.

Cross, K. (2004) 'Engagement and excitement in mathematics', *Mathematics Teaching*, 189: 4–6.

Dehaene, S. (1997) *The Number Sense*. Oxford: Oxford University Press.

Department for Education and Employment (DfEE) (1999) *The National Numeracy Strategy: Information for Governors*. London: DfEE.

Desforges, C. (1985) 'Matching tasks to children's attainments', in Bennett, N. and Desforges, C. (eds) *Recent Advances in Classroom Research*. Edinburgh: Scottish Academic Press.

DfEE (1999) *All Our Futures: National Advisory Committee for Creativity and Culture in Education Report*. London: DfEE.

DfES (2000) *The National Curriculum*. London: DfES.

DfES (2003) *Excellence and Enjoyment: A Strategy for Primary Schools*. Nottingham: DfES.

DfES (2004) *Primary National Strategy: Learning to Learn*. London: DfES.

Duffy, B. (1998) *Supporting Creativity and Imagination in the Early Years*. Maidenhead: Open University Press.

Eames, A., Benton, T., Sharp, C. and Kendall, L. (2006) *The Impact of Creative Partnerships on the Attainment of Young People*. Slough: NFER.

Ernest, P. (2000) 'Teaching and learning mathematics', in Koshy, V., Ernest, P., and Casey, R. *Mathematics for Primary Teachers*. London: Routledge.

Fisher, R. and Williams, M. (eds) (2004) *Unlocking Creativity: Teaching Across the Curriculum*. London: David Fulton.

Gardner, H. (1993) *Creating Minds, An Anatomy of Creativity Seen Through the Lives of Freud, Einstein, Picasso, Stravinsky, Eliot, Graham and Gandhi*. New York: Dutton.

Glennon, V.J. (1963) 'Some Perspectives in Education', in *Enrichment Mathematics for the Grades* (27th Yearbook). Washington DC: National Council of Teachers of Mathematics.

Gray, E. and Pitta, D. (1997) 'Changing Emily's images'. *Mathematics Teaching*, 161: 48–51.

Halliwell, S. (1993) 'Teacher creativity and teacher education', in Bridges, D. and Kerry, T. (eds) *Developing Teachers Professionally; Reflections for Initial and In-service Trainers*. London: Routledge, pp. 67–78.

Hardy, G.H. (1941) *A Mathematician's Apology*. London: Cambridge University Press.

Haury, D.L. (2001) *Literature-based Mathematics in Elementary School*. Washington, DC: National Association for Gifted Children.

Hershkowitz, R. (1989) 'Visualization in geometry: two sides of the coin', *Focus on Learning Problems in Mathematics*, 11(1–2): 61–76.

Hong, H. (1996). 'Effects of mathematics learning through children's literature on math achievement and dispositional outcomes'. *Early Childhood Research Quarterly*, 11(4): 477–494.

Hughes, M. (1999) 'The National Numeracy Strategy: are we getting it right?', *The Psychology of Education Review*, 23(2): 3–7.

Jeffrey, B. and Woods, P. (2003) *The Creative School: A Framework for Success, Quality and Effectiveness*. London: RoutledgeFalmer.

King, J. (1992) *The Art of Mathematics*. New York and London: Plenum Press.

Loeman, M.-T. (2002) *How to learn from and make history in maths*. Available: www.xtec.es/vs/mathematics/tmathexc/.

Meissner, H. (2000) 'Creativity in mathematics education', in *Proceedings of the Mathematics Education Study Group (MESG)*, August 7–8. Tokyo, Japan.

Meyer, R.E. (1999) 'Fifty years of creativity research', in Sternberg, R.J. (ed) *Handbook of Creativity*. New York: Cambridge University Press, pp. 449–460.

Miller, R.C. (1990) *Discovering Mathematical Talent*. Washington, DC: National Association for Gifted Children.

National Advisory Committee on Creative and Cultural Education (NACCCE) (1999) *All Our Futures: Creativity, Culture and Education*. Suffolk: DfEE (The Robinson Report).

National Curriculum Council (1989) *Mathematics: Non-Statutory Guidance*. York: NCC/HMSO.

Ofsted (2000) *Teaching of literacy and mathematics in reception classes: A survey by HMI*. Available: www.ofsted.gov.uk.

Ofsted (2003) *Expecting the unexpected*. HMI 1612. Available: www.ofsted.gov.uk.

Ofsted (2006) *The Annual Report of Her Majesty's Chief Inspector of Schools 2005/06*. Available: www.ofsted.gov.uk.

Ofsted (2007) *The foundation stage: A survey of 144 settings*. Available: www.ofsted.gov.uk.

Oussoren, R.A. (2000) *Write Dance*. London: PCP.

Policastro, E. and Gardner, H. (1999) 'From case studies to robust generalizations, an approach to the study of creativity', in Sternberg, R.J. (ed) *Handbook of Creativity*. New York: Cambridge University Press, pp. 213–225.

Porter, L. (2005) *Gifted Young Children (2nd Edition): A Guide for Teachers and Parents*. Berkshire: Open University Press.

Pratt, D. (1995) 'Young children's interpretation of experiments mediated through active and passive graphing', *Journal of Computer Assisted Learning*, 11: 157–169.

QCA/DfES (2000) *Curriculum Guidance for the Foundation Stage*. London: QCA/DfES.

QCA (2000) *Mathematics Key Stage 2, Test A, Levels 3–5*. London: QCA.

QCA (2004) *Creativity: Find It, Promote It. Promoting Children's Creative Thinking and Behaviours Across the Curriculum at Key Stages 1, 2 and 3*. Suffolk: QCA.

Robinson, D. and Koshy, V. (2004) 'Creative mathematics: allowing caged birds to fly', in Fisher, R. and Williams, M. (eds) *Unlocking Creativity: Teaching Across the Curriculum*. London: David Fulton, pp. 68–81.

Rogoff, B. and Lave, J. (1984) *Everyday Cognition: Its Development in Social Context*. Harvard, MA: Harvard University Press.

Scottish Executive (2000) *The Scottish Cultural Strategy: Creating our Future . . . Minding our Past*. Scotland: Scottish Executive.

Sharp, C. (2004) 'Developing young children's creativity: what can we learn from research', *Topic*, 32: 5–12.

Singh, S. (1997) *Fermat's Last Theorem: The Story of the Riddle that Confounded the World's Greatest Minds for 358 Years*. London: Fourth Estate.

Skemp, R. (1979) *Intelligence, Learning and Action*. Chichester: John Wiley and Sons.

Stein, M.I. (1984) *Stimulating Creativity, Vol 1: Individual Procedures*. New York: Academic Press.

Takahashi, A. (2006) Characteristics of Japanese Mathematics Lessons. Available: www.criced.tsukuba.ac.jp/math/sympo_2006/takahashi.pdf.

Tall, D., Gray, E., Bin Ali, M., Crowley, L., DeMarois, P., McGowen, M., Pitta, D., Pinto, M., Thomas, M. and Yusof, Y. (2001) 'Symbols and the bifurcation between procedural and conceptual thinking', *Canadian Journal of Mathematics and Technology Education*, 1(1): 81–104.

Tegano, D.W., Moran, J.D. and Sawyers, J.K. (1991). *Creativity in Early Childhood Classrooms* (NEA Early Childhood Education Series). West Haven, CT: National Education Association.

Tobias, S. (undated) *Fostering Creativity in Science and Mathematics Classrooms*. Available: www.wpi.edu/News/Events/SENM/tobias.ppt.

Turner, S. and McCullouch, J. (2004) *Making Connections in Primary Mathematics*. London: David Fulton.

Usnick, V. and McCarthy, J. (1998). 'Turning adolescents onto mathematics through literature', *Middle School Journal* 29 (4): 50–54.

Waller, W. (1932) *The Sociology of Teaching*. New York: Wiley.

Welchman-Tischler, R. (1992) *How to use children's literature to teach mathematics*. Reston, VA: National Council of Teachers of Mathematics. Available: watt.enc.org/online/ENC2285/2285.html.

Willings, D. (1980) *The Creatively Gifted – Recognising and Developing the Creative Personality*. Cambridge: Woodhead Faulkner.

Wilson, K. and Briggs, M. (2002) 'Able and gifted: judging by appearances?', *Mathematics Teaching*, 180: 34–36.

Woods, P. (1990) *Teacher Skills and Strategies*. Lewes: Falmer Press.

Woods, P. (1995) *Creative Teachers in Primary Schools*. Buckingham: Open University Press.

Yoshida, M. (2005) 'Using lesson study to develop effective blackboard practice', in Wang-Iverson, P. and Yoshida, M. (eds), *Building our Understanding of Lesson Study*. Philadelphia, PA: Research for Better Schools, pp. 93–100.

Further reading

Craft, A. with Dyer, G., Dugal, J., Jeffrey, R. and Lyons, T. (1997) *Can You Teach Creativity?* Nottingham: Ed Now Books.

Craft, A. (2000) *Creativity across the Primary Curriculum*. London: Routledge.

Fisher, R. and Williams, M. (eds) (2004) *Unlocking Creativity: Teaching across the Curriculum*. London: David Fulton.

Uptitis, R., Phillips, E. and Higginson, W. (1997) *Creative Mathematics: Exploring Children's Understanding*. New York: Routledge.

Wilson, A. (ed) (2005) *Creativity in Primary Education*. Exeter: Learning Matters.

www.enrich.maths.org.

www.qca.org.uk.

Index

Note: page numbers in italics denote figures or tables

able/gifted children 15, 18–19, 140
accountability 34–5, 37, 144
addition, dice-throwing 49
adult support 52–3
affective domain 88–9
Agincourt, Battle of 92
Alcuin 94, 102
algebra 6
Alice in Wonderland 71
answers, arriving at 17–18, 19, 20–1
art and mathematics *130*
art galleries 128–9
Askew, M. 29, 89
assessment of mathematical writing 96–8
Austin, P. 69
Avital, S. 94

Babbage, C. 122
Barker, J. 92
Be Very Afraid website 66, 142–3
bean-growing 50
BECTA project 142
bee teams 67
behaviourist approach 29
Bennett, N. 47
Benton, T. 138
Bidwell, J. 94
Bjorkqvist, O. 142
books, hand-made 120
bows and arrows 92, *93*
Briggs, M. 4, 49, 54
Brown, M. 29
Bruce, T. 3, 42
builder's yard 60
Burton, L. 57, 67

calculating devices 122

calculation 6, 27, 62, *83*
calculators 143
calendar numbers 87, 119
Canaletto 129
Charlottes Web (White) 77
child-centred approach 141
children's involvement 125–8, 145
children's literature: *see* storybooks
Christmas party planning 51
class discussion *9*, 85–6
classification of objects 4, 5–6
classroom tasks, typology 47
Coles, D. 42–3
collections and containers *55*, 58
combinatorix problem 70
communication 31, 33–4
computer use, graphing 143
confidence 144
Connect Four 108
connectionist approach 30
Constable, J. 129
context, real-life 43
control, curriculum 8
cooking activities 128
co-ordinator role 121–2
Copeland, T. 42–3
counting tasks 6, 69–70
Craft, A. 7
Creative Partnerships 137–9
creative thinking 21–2, 31, 32
creativity: classroom examples 38–9;
    definition 1–3; difficulties 19–21; in Early
    Years 15, 16; and employability 35; layers of
    3–4; in learning 7, *14*; mathematics 4–6, *14*,
    15, 23–4; planning 144–5; play 5–6; prob-
    lem solving 3; Scottish Education 2; of
    teachers 10, 16

Creativity: find it (QCA) 22, 34
Cropley, A.J. 2, 22
cross-curricular learning 25, 28, 36–7, 42–3, 50, 89, 121
curriculum 8, 25–8

darts 108
data handling 54, 143
Deal or No Deal 110
Desforges, C. 47
DfEE 29
DfEE/QCA 23
dice 49, 55
differentiation 52
discovery approach 30
display 9; activities 116; co-ordinator role 121–2; creating 111–15; outdoors 122–4; as stimulus 115–20
dominoes 45, 55, 106–7

Eames, A. 138
Early Learning Goals 27
Early Years 15, 16, 25–6, 49
editorial teams 67
Edward II 130
Egyptians 62–3
Einstein, A. 2–3
elephant teams 67
English Heritage 91
Ephialtes 77
Ernest, P. 139
evaluation 31, 33
Every Child Matters 34–5, 68, 144
Excellence and Enjoyment 25, 30–1
experimentation 16
explorations 128–31

facilitating 142
felt walls 120
Fermat, P. de 3, 23, *90*, 91
field trips 125–8
films/role-play 66
Finnish study 142
flower shop 60
Foundation Stage 25–6
French Revolution *93*, 94
fruit salad game 100
fuel consumption 126

game show television 109
game-playing 5–6
games: adapting 99–100, 101–2; developments from 109; for journey 126–7; outdoors 123
garden centre 60

Gardner, H. 2
German project 140
Glennon, Y. 7
Goldilocks and the Three Bears 70
government website 27
graphs 25, 50, 143
Greece, Ancient 64–5
group activities, role-play 54
groupings 53
'Guess who I am?' game 101, 102

haberdashery 59
Halliwell, S. 9
handshakes problem 104–5, *106*
Harry Potter and the Philosopher's Stone 71
health and safety 60, 127
Henry V 92
Heppell, S. 66
history and mathematics 91–4
holiday planning 51
Hong, H. 69
hopscotch 108
Hughes, M. 28
humour 18, 70

ice cream van 60
ICT 142, 145
indoors and outdoors learning 26
information processing 31, 32–3
initial training of new teachers 37
innovation 8, 137
Integrated Learning System 54
investigations 9, 22, 130–1
Irons, C. 71
Irons, R. R. 71
IWBs *54*, 141, 145

Japanese study 140–1
Jeffrey, B. 38
Jim and the Beanstalk 70, 72–3
Johnson, D. 29
Josephus, Flavius 105–6
journaling 33, 88–9

Kendall, L. 138
kinaesthetic learning *9*, 54
Kingscourt storybooks 68, 70, 71
knowledge 15, 16
Kovalevskaya, Sofia 111

language development 4–5
Lave, J. 30
learning 10, 11, 27–8
Learning and Development 25, 26–7

learning environment 42, 115
length *83*
Leonardo da Vinci 3
Leonidas, King 77
Loeman, M.-T. 140
logic puzzles 44, 102–4
loop cards 45, 107
Lovelace, A. 122
Lucas, E. 105

McCullouch, J. 43
Mantle of the Expert 65
Mastermind 109–10
Matching Green school 66
mathematical thinking 6
mathematical writing 96–8
mathematicians 64–5, 89–90, 122
mathematics: creativity 4–6, *14*, 15, 23–4; curriculum 25–8; and history 91–4; history of 94; image problem 22–3; rules 13; stereotypes 139; utilitarian 36; writing in 82, *83*, 84–5
mathematics teaching 7–10, 13, 15, 27, 31, 32
mathematics trails 131, 133–6
mazes 107, *108*
measurement 27, 51, 62–3, 116
Megamaths Multiplication video 117
Meissner, H. 140
Meyer, R.E. 2
Miller, R.C. 140
Milton Keynes Museum 131
mobile technology 142–3, 145
mobiles, hanging 117
Mondrian, P. 130
money samples 41
Moran, J.D. 138
multiples 106–7
multiplication 45, 49
museums 130–1, *132*

NACCCE (National Advisory Committee on Creative and Cultural Education) 10, 14, 138
National Curriculum 26, 30, 31
National Gallery 129
National Numeracy Framework 27, 28–9
National Numeracy Strategy 6, 37, 51, 117
National Treasure 66
natural world 131
Night at the Museum 77–8
noises 5–6
Northampton Museum and Art Gallery 130
number associations 87, *88*, 112, 124
number collections 119–20
number concepts 27, 45, 68–9, 143

number lines 117
number patterns 45, 85–6, 123
number sacks 40–1
number spider 115, 119
number squares 123
number tracks 117–18
numeracy 25

Ofsted 10, 25, 27, 28, 55, 137
100 square 115, 118–19
Oussoren, R.A. 39–40
ownership 8, 36
Oxfam resources for teachers 75
Oxford Reading Tree 71

palindromic numbers 86
parcels *55*
participant/personal response system 109
pattern-making 26
peer assessment 33
people mathematics 116, 123–4
personalised learning 10, 36, 144
physical education *9*
physical environment 91–2
picnic activities 57–9
PISA studies 142
play 5, 6, 15
Playground EU project 142
Policastro, E. 2
population figures *84*
post office 60
posters 115
practical activities 26, 49, 51; display 116; outdoors 42, 122–4
Pratt, D. 143
prediction 5–6
pre-school children 4–5
Primary National Strategy 11, 30–8, 121, 140, 144
problem solving: creativity 3; cross-curricular work 42–3; Japanese study 140–1; practical activities 26, 51; teaching of 15, 27, 31, 32; visualisation 22
problem types 94, 95–6; *see also specific named problems*

QCA, *Creativity: find it* 22, 34
QTS 37
quantities 4
The Queen's Knickers 70
question/answer game 45

Raiders of the Lost Ark 66
reading schemes 71

reasoning 31, 33, 97–8
recording 6, 53
reinforcement of concepts 117
relay teams 45
Relic Hunter 66
resources 40, 53, 55, 61, 145
Rhind papyrus puzzle 64
Rhodes, V. 29
river-crossing problem 102–4
The Roberts' Report, Nurturing Creativity in Young People 34
Robinson Report 14
Rogoff, B. 30
role-play 54, 56–61, 66, 67
routinisation 36, 47
Rugby Museum 131

sandwich making 51, 57–8
sausage rolls 58
Sawyer, J.K. 138
scaled objects 43–4
scoring, calculating 62
Scottish Education 2
Scottish Executive 2, 4
self-assessment 33
self-esteem 99
Senet 63–4
shapes 67, 124
Sharp, C. 13, 14, 138
Shoe Museum, Street 131
shoes 59, 130–1
shop windows 116
shopping 55, 59–61, 128, *129*
The Snowman 70
Somerville, M. 122
sorting activities 49
space 22, 67
spiders 77
sport 87
Stanley Bagshaw and the Short-sighted Goalkeeper 70
Stein, M.I. 2
storybooks 40–1, 68–9, *75, 78–81*
subject knowledge 16, 144
supermarket 59, 128

Takahashi, A. 140–1
Tall, D. 19
Tate Gallery 130
teachers 7–10, 29, 37–8
teaching strategies 44–5
teams in role-play 67
technology, types *54,* 66, 142–3

Tegano, D.W. 138
television 66, *76*
tenpin bowling 61–2
tessellation 113
300 film 77
Thermopylae, Battle of 77
thinking skills 1, 21
tiddlywinks 108
time concepts 91–2, 145
Tobias, S. 139, 140
Tomb Raider 66
topic approach 11, 25, 38
Tower of Hanoi 105
toys 6, *55*
train timetables 41
trainee teachers 46–7
transmission 29
travel agency 59–60
travel information box 41
travel sickness 127
treasure hunts 66
Turner, S. 42–3

Victoria and Albert Museum 131
visualisation 22
Visumath 142
vocabulary for mathematics 4, 26, 86, 116

Waller, W. 36
washing lines 116, 120
Weakest Link 110
website use *54*
weighing 58
Welchman-Tischler, R. 69, 74
White, E.B. 77
Who wants to be a millionaire? 109
Wiles, A. 3, 23
Wiliam, D. 29
Willings, D. 21
Woods, P. 8, 36, 38, 45
word problems 95–6
worksheets: as control 8; Early Years 49; limitations 46, 47–9; National Numeracy Strategy 6; trainee teachers 46–7
world trip 65
write dance 39–40
writing, teaching of 39–40
writing frame 98
writing in mathematics 82, *83,* 84–5

Xerxes 77

Yoshido, M. 140–1